Becoming His
A Year-Long Bible Study for Christian Women

Courtnye Jackson

Copyright © 2019 Courtnye Jackson

All Rights Reserved. No part of this publication may be reproduced, stored in a retrieval system, or transmitted, in any form or by any means, electronic, mechanical, photocopying, recording or otherwise.

Scripture quotations are from the ESV® Bible (The Holy Bible, English Standard Version®), copyright © 2001 by Crossway Bibles, a publishing ministry of Good News Publishers. Used by permission. All rights reserved."

Editor Elizabeth Smith

Dedication

This book is dedicated to my God who gave me life & my wonderful parents who showed me what it means to truly live for Christ

"Women were created from the rib of man to be beside him, not from his head to top him, nor from his feet to be trampled by him, but from under his arm to be protected by him, near to his heart to be loved by him."

Matthew Henry: *An Exposition of the Old and New Testament*

I am so glad you decided to take the journey of Becoming His! It is going to be quite an adventure, and one that comes with many rewards. I wrote Becoming His because I was seeking a Bible study that focused on biblical marriage while keeping Christ and godly womanhood at the forefront.

Throughout the next 49 weeks prepare to grow in and understand many of the qualities and characteristics of a godly woman based on scriptural standards and hence a godly wife.

I created this book with the thought of fellowship in mind, but time is also allowed for individual processing, as we all have various learning styles. It is ideal if you have (or can create) a monthly Bible study to work in small groups together. The small Bible study groups are so you can bounce ideas off each other, quiz each other on the Scriptures for the month, and simply have a good time becoming.

When you plan to study by yourself, make sure you set aside a specific amount of time daily to get through the Scriptures and readings. Take the time to understand what the Scriptures are saying and what they mean to you in your life. Pick them apart and make notes around them.

It's important that you are connecting with God daily through reading His Word and through prayer. Find an accountability partner or prayer partner from your group or do group accountability. God's Word is our guide through life; it is our daily sustenance.

As a Christian woman, I have learned that my walk with God is important in all areas of life. If I wish to be a godly wife, I must first be a godly single woman. The traits and characteristics I practice and perfect in my single life will ultimately transfer to marriage. Learning these things is a lot easier while single, so I don't want to waste my single life too focused on one small aspect of it. The best thing you can do for your future family is to form a deep, committed relationship and bond with God. A godly wife knows that no matter how much she wants a marriage, she is not going to jeopardize her relationship with God for earthly pleasure.

As godly wives, we have already taken on this role well before we say, "I do." We carry ourselves as already taken and know that we are to be found by our godly husbands at some point, if this is God's desire.

Just a couple of things before you start, don't beat yourself up if you stop and start. It's a lot of ground to cover and life happens, just pick back up where you left off. Take your time and really focus on the questions asked so you can answer them honestly and thoughtfully. Lastly, if I have learned nothing else in my forty-something years on earth, it's that application is the key to success. In other words, if you have knowledge but don't put it to work, it isn't going to work for you. So, delve in, but make sure you do the work and take it seriously.

Most of all have fun!

God Bless,

Court

HOW TO USE THIS GUIDE

THE PARTS OF THE GUIDE:

READINGS	These can be done prior to your group Bible study, or time can be allotted during the meeting (10–15 mins).
GROUP QUESTIONS	These should be answered during the group Bible study (15-20 mins).
GROUP ACTIVITIES	This activity should be done during your group Bible study. Allot 20-30 minutes.
WEEKLY MEMORIZATION SCRIPTURE	Take some time to meditate and memorize this Scripture throughout the week. How can you apply it to your own life and use it to strengthen your relationship with God? There is also a section to SOAP the scripture in the *Becoming His Journal*.
WEEKLY SCRIPTURE QUESTIONS	These are to be done individually. Take the time to be thoughtful about your answers. They can be shared with the group if you desire after you have answered them on your own.
WEEKLY ACTIVITY	These should be done individually and can take anywhere from one hour to a couple of days. It is recommended that you take your time in doing them and come back to them throughout the week.
WEEKLY PRAYER	This is a prayer you should focus on; it is recommended that you write each one out and refer back to them.
SUPPLEMENTAL SCRIPTURES	These Scriptures can be found at the bottom of the page and will supplement the weekly memorization Scripture. You can also meditate on these!
MONTHLY CHECK-IN	The first and the last question are always the same but still should be answered and used to track your growth. These check-ins can be shared at your group—in fact, it is recommended that you share some form of testimony from the month with your group for encouragement and edification!

THINGS YOU WILL NEED FOR EACH ACTIVITY:

	Activity	Items
1	Create my life	- 2 sheets of paper - 1 pen per person
2	God's Plan	- 2 sheets of paper - 1 pen per person
3	Plan to Serve	- 2 sheets of paper - 1 pen per person - Internet access
4	Overcome	- 2 sheets of paper - 1 pen per person
5	Testimony Time	- 2 sheets of paper - 1 pen per person
6	Ask, Believe, Receive	- Glue - One board per person - Old magazines: 3–5 per person - Internet access and printer, if available - Printed photos of things you want in your life - Scissors
7	What I like About Me	- 1 pen per person
8	Forgiven	- 2 sheets of paper - 1 pen per person
9	Date Night	- 2 sheets of paper - 1 pen per person
10	Circle of love	- Pack of sticky notes - 1 pen per person
11	31 Ways	- Pens
12	Give Yourself Away	- Bonfire material, balloon release

SOME THINGS YOU MAY WANT TO CONSIDER BEFORE YOU GET STARTED:

- Meet in a comfortable location where you are free to talk, laugh and express yourself
- Establish study-group rules at the initial meeting
    - This is a safe space to share and be open; nothing leaves the group.
    - Ideally, a different person should lead prayer every session—this is important especially so that people who are quiet, like myself, contribute.
    - A leader is also needed for each session to prepare for the next month's group activity so that you don't have to look ahead. A list of items you will need for each activity can be found on the following pages.
- Don't skip the monthly check-ins, they ensure your progress and can be done with your group or on your own.
- I encourage you not to look ahead at the activities or upcoming months.
- Keep a calendar of how much time you spend with God each day, check it off, and put the time next to it. You can download a free journaling calendar and prayer sheets that go along with this book at: www.becominghisministries.com.
- Keep a journal. You can purchase the 'Becoming His' Journal from our website or use one you already have on hand
- Connecting more than once a month for a very brief time (10-15 mins), consider the following:
    - Have a weekly prayer call
    - Have an online brief check in
    - Have a conference call every other week just to catch up
- Be open and honest
- Allow time for everyone to speak, if it is a very passionate subject use a 'talking stick'; this is an item that can be passed to the person speaking. When they are speaking, everyone is listening. This ensures everyone gets a say.
- Enjoy yourself and the journey, if you do please leave a good review for this study and share with others to encourage them on their journeys!

Table of Contents

She Is a Woman of God 1
She Keeps God First 19
She Has a Servants Heart 35
She Is Strong 51
She Establishes Her Temple 68
She Builds Her Home 86
She Brings Her Husband Good 102
She Is Weak 120
She Understands There Is More 136
She Finds Her Tribe 154
She Is a Woman of Excellence 170
She Is Busy About Her Father's Work 188

One

SHE IS A GODLY WOMAN

Month One

An excellent wife, who can find?
For her worth is far above jewels

Proverbs 31:10

Taking on the role of a godly wife comes second to being a woman of God. Throughout your marriage, the best thing a wife can do is remain close to God. All the women you will learn and read about throughout this time are godly women, but the women you read about in the following passages have a vital quality of godly wives. They both said yes to God's will in their lives above anyone else's, including their own.

READINGS

- Judges 13
- Luke 1:26–38

Group Questions

1. What are some similarities you recognize between Manoah's wife's and Mary's stories?

   _____
   _____
   _____

2. What are these women's responses to God's request?

   _____
   _____
   _____

3. Have you ever found yourself procrastinating with what God asks of you or simply saying no? How does/did it make you feel? How can you ensure that you will follow God's directive for your life going forward?

4. When Manoah's wife encounters the angel, her husband is the first person she runs to tell. What are some ways you would describe Manoah's wife's interaction with her husband? (For example, does she seem respectful or needy?) How can you take some of these qualities and use them when you marry?

5. What knowledge can you gain about faith and fear from these stories?

6. What is your definition of a godly woman? Would you describe the women in these stories as godly women?

GROUP ACTIVITY: Create My Life

Complete the "best life" questionnaire below. Answer the questions as specifically as you can. Really give it your attention and be detailed! Share with others in your group if you desire. (Question 9 is for anything else you would like to add.)

1. Close your eyes and think of your husband walking through the door. What does he look like? How does he respond and interact with you? If you desire children, how does he interact with the family? Write down some of the characteristics you desire in a mate.

2. How many children do you want to have?

3. Where do you want to live?

4. What type of work do you want to do? Will you be a stay-at-home mom, entrepreneur, doctor, or work for a company?

5. How much money do you want to make?

6. What type of car would you like to have?

7. Describe your dream home. Be specific! How many bathrooms does it have? How big is the yard (if there is one)? Are there two or three levels? What view do you see when you look out the window in the morning?

8. Describe your dream wedding: colors, venue, number of bridesmaids, etc.

9.

WEEK ONE

SHE ABIDES IN GOD

Above all, a godly wife recognizes that without God she is nothing and the best thing she can do for her marriage is to remain in Him. The definition of *abide* is to remain stable or fixed in a state, meaning that we are to remain with God. In the Bible, Jesus is described as the vine and we as the branches; the branches cannot survive apart from its life source, the vine. We cannot survive apart from Him; our spirit will remain malnourished. We are to seek Him as a source for everything, especially marriage. First John 2:6 says, "Whoever claims to live in him must live as Jesus did."

Scripture Memorization

John 15:4 – Abide in me, and I in you. As the branch cannot bear fruit by itself, unless it abides in the vine, neither can you, unless you abide in me.

Reflection Questions

1. John tells us that if we abide in Him, we are to walk like Him, and if we keep His commands, we will abide in Him. What other benefits of abiding in Christ does the Bible state?

2. How do we draw near to God? How do we seek Him?

3. What does your life look like abiding in Christ?

4. What does abiding together as a couple look like to you?

ACTIVITY: PLANT A DREAM!

Journal prompt: I feel discontent in my journey when…

Materials needed: Seeds, dirt, pots

This week find the time to plant a dream! Dreams are like plants—you plant them with an idea, you water them, feed them, shelter them, care for them, and watch them grow.

Make sure the plant is small enough to keep close to you every day, perhaps sitting on your desk or nightstand, but where you will be able to focus on it throughout this journey to remind you that you are planting dreams!

Our dreams and desires are much like seeds we plant—they need the right environment, consistent care, and time to grow. Keep the plant somewhere you will see it as a reminder to yourself when you get frustrated that your dreams are still growing, they are taking root, and eventually, you will begin to see the fruit of your labor and prayers.

Pray for joy and contentment

2 John 1:9 | John 15:7 | 1 John 2:6 | 1 John 2:28

WEEK TWO

SHE IS A PRAYER WARRIOR

Prayer is one of the most important aspects of the Christian walk. It is how we communicate with God and how He hears our petitions. There isn't just one way to pray. In the Bible, we see many ways. Hannah (1 Sam. 1:9–14) prayed with her lips moving, but no sound coming out. Many others in the Bible even pray through song, and God hears them. Jesus gave us an outline of prayer in Matthew 7:15. Take some time to really read over the prayer and see the key parts. As a godly wife, prayer should be our number one go-to in life when things are both going well and when they aren't.

Scripture Memorization

1 Thessalonians 5:17 – Pray without ceasing

Reflection Questions

- Look at the times it was stated in the Bible that Jesus went into prayer. What was going on at that time? What was He facing?

- How does the Holy Spirit help us in our prayer life?

- Why is prayer so important in your Christian walk?

- What are some benefits of prayer per the Bible? Pull out specific Scriptures.

- What type of prayer life do you want to have with your husband?

ACTIVITY: PRAYER LIST

Journal prompt: *I don't always pray for others because…*

Make a prayer list of seven people; pray for one person each day!

Name	Prayer

Ask God who and what He wants you to pray for and write it above.

Philippians 4:6 | Mark 11:24 | Romans 8:26 | Matthew 6:6–7

WEEK THREE

SHE IS A KINGDOM SEEKER

A godly wife is a woman after God's own heart. She seeks for righteousness and the kingdom of God. The Bible tells us that those who do righteousness all the time are blessed and that we are righteous as He is righteous. As women of God, one of our focuses is to pursue and exhibit righteousness as Christians.

Scripture Memorization

Matthew 6:33 – But seek first the kingdom of God and his righteousness, and all these things will be added to you.

Reflection Questions

- What exactly is the kingdom of God? Find other passages in the Bible that support your theory.

- How do you seek God's righteousness? Who are some righteous people in the Bible?

- What exactly is righteousness and how can we embody and seek it?

ACTIVITY: RIGHTEOUSNESS

Journal prompt:
Practicing righteousness can help me in marriage by…

How would you describe the actions of a righteous person? Write down as many actions and attributes as you can think of—if you can find some in the Bible! Include how a righteous person acts when angry, irritated, and sad.

This week, focus on truly being and living a righteous life. Take the list you created and apply it to your life. Use the chart on the next page to keep a log of your successes and failures. Don't beat yourself up if you aren't always successful, but acknowledge yourself for seeing the need for change and self-reflection. Reflect on why you missed the mark. Try to stick with it for the whole month.

Daily journal prompt: Keep track of when you made or missed the mark of acting righteously. Note in what ways you notice an improvement in yourself or how you could have done better.

Pray for God to show you where you aren't being righteous in life

1 John 3:7 | Psalm 106:3 | Isaiah 33:15–17 | 1 Peter 3:14

ATTRIBUTES OF A RIGHTEOUS PERSON

1.

2.

3.

4.

5.

6.

7.

8.

9.

10.

WEEK 4

SHE DOES NOT LOVE THE WORLD

While a godly woman and wife loves the people of the world, she does not love what the world offers. She is focused on heavenly things as instructed by her Father above. Her eyes are set on things eternal, not of this world. Yes, she may have money, cars, a family, and a fabulous job; but those things do not have her, nor does she place them above God.

Scripture Memorization

1 John 2:15 – Do not love the world or the things in the world. If anyone loves the world, the love of the Father is not in him.

Reflection Questions

1. Why do you suppose that if you love the things of the world, the love of the Father is not in you?

2. What does it look like to be a lover of things of this world?

3. Where do you think marriage and family fit into this Scripture? Are they of this world?

ACTIVITY: A BEAUTIFUL REFLECTION

This week take some time to reflect on your love of the world. What do you desire, possess, or seek that may be displeasing to God because of your heart attachments? What things come before God and His desires for your life? Is there anything in your life that you could not see living without? Make a list of the things that come to mind and pray over them nightly. Discuss one of the things with your group.

Journal reflection: When it comes to not loving the world, I have a difficult time…

Pray for God to reveal your heart toward things of this world

1 John 2:16–17 I 1 John 3:1 I Matthew 6:24 I 1 John 5:19

Monthly Check-in

Did I connect with God regularly this month?

How do I improve for next month?

What is my strategy for becoming a woman after God's own heart?

Is there anything positive that has occurred as a result of my studies or closer connection with God this month?

TESTIMONY TO SHARE:

Notes

Two

SHE KEEPS GOD FIRST

Month Two

Charm is deceptive, and beauty is fleeting; but a woman who fears the Lord is to be praised

Proverbs 31:30

The following passages are about two well-known women seen throughout the Bible in various passages. Building a relationship with God is at the core of a godly wife's priorities. Although the women in the following passages are sisters, they seem to be quite different. Their story is a great example of putting and keeping God first.

READINGS

- Luke 10:38–42
- John 11

GROUP QUESTIONS

1. Throughout the readings, we get a pretty good idea of some differing characteristics Mary and Martha embodied. What are some major differences you can pull out of their stories? Are these qualities of godly women?

   _____
   _____
   _____
   _____
   _____
   _____

2. In Luke 10, we are introduced to the sisters, Mary and Martha, who obviously have different priorities. In your own words write what Jesus tells Martha in verses 41 and 42.

   _____
   _____
   _____

3. When people saw Mary jump up in a hurry, they assumed she was overcome with a grief so strong that she had to go to the tomb to cry there, but she was really running to Jesus. When in a tough situation, where is the first place you usually run to and why?

   _____
   _____
   _____

4. Although we cannot sit at the Lord's feet today and listen to His teachings as Mary did, we do get directives from Him through the Bible. How often do you read your Bible each week?

   _____
   _____

5. Thinking of your day-to-day life, do you think Jesus would place you in the Martha category or the Mary category? Why?

   _____
   _____
   _____
   _____
   _____

6. What can you take about putting God first from these two women and apply in your own life? What can you eventually apply to your marriage?

   _____
   _____
   _____
   _____
   _____
   _____

NOTES

Group Activity: God's Plan

Even after you get married, the best thing you can do for your family is to keep God first and foremost in your life and relationships. To do this, you must continue to cultivate the practices of seeking Him with all your heart. We don't seek God to get things from Him. We shouldn't use Him like a genie; He won't allow that. The promises of God aren't why we draw near to Him, but to have a genuine relationship and delight in His presence is what we should focus on. That way, even if things don't turn out according to our plans, we won't become bitter or angry, and will continue in our relationship with him.

Create a God-plan you will follow today and continue throughout your life. Granted, it will be altered as life goes on, but try to establish a routine you will follow and can see yourself sticking with now, one you will be accustomed to prior to entering a relationship. Write down when, how long, and where you will do each activity.

Put the activities on your calendar or your phone and set reminders for yourself. As creatures of habit, eventually it will become like second nature to spend quality time with God regularly—as it should!

> Take it further: Create or download a Bible reading plan to follow as well.

MY GOD-PLAN

Activity	How long	When	Where	Other
Prayer				
Study				
Sit quietly				
Meditate on Scripture				
Intercede for others				
Journal				

WEEK FIVE

SHE POSSESSES THE FEAR OF GOD

Several times throughout the Bible you are told to fear God, but it is not the type of fear we may be thinking of. The word *fear* in these Scriptures is derived from Hebrew *yare'*, which can mean "to fear or reverence." When you read through the Bible, you sometimes see that if someone was in God's presence, they fell on their faces. First Kings 18:38–39 and Numbers 20:6 are two examples of showing reverence for God's greatness. We learn that the fear of God is the beginning of wisdom in Proverbs 9:10; it is the hatred of evil and the fountain of youth! The fear of God is at the core of the Christian walk.

Scripture Memorization

Proverbs 31:30 (ESV) — Charm is deceitful, and beauty is vain, but a woman who fears the Lord is to be praised.

Reflection Questions

1. In Exodus 20:20 Moses says that having the fear of God will keep the people from sinning. To understand what the fear of the Lord is, we must look to the Bible. Find at least three or more Scriptures that explain what the fear of the Lord is.

2. Do you feel like you possess the fear of the Lord? Do your everyday actions express your reverence toward Him? If yes, why? If not, why do you not feel as if this is something you do?

3. Why do you think God wants you to fear Him?

4. How do you think having the fear of God will assist you in having healthy relationships?

ACTIVITY: SETTING BOUNDARIES

JOURNAL PROMPT: *The fear of God means to me...*

How do you plan to continue to keep God first after He has presented your husband to you? What things will you do to ensure your relationship with Him does not fall by the wayside and you are still being obedient to Him first and foremost? For example, what boundaries will you put in place when dating? How will you find time to still study and pray? Will you do this together? Will you have a prayer closet after marriage?

Make a list of some ways you will do this with your significant other. In what ways do you think you can do these things as a couple? Share this with your study group and exchange ideas.

Pray to understand and seek the fear of God

Proverbs 1:7 I Proverbs 8:13 I Ecclesiastes 12:13 I Psalm 33:8 I Psalm 128:1-3

WEEK SIX

SHE IS OBEDIENT

As Christian wives we are called to be submissive to our husbands but obedient to God even after marriage. If your husband asks you to do something that goes against the will of God, you take that to his Head—God! In Acts 5:29 we are told that we must obey God instead of men. Obedience is sometimes like a dirty word in a world that seems to praise rebellion, but God requires obedience of us and states that if we love Him, we will obey Him (John 14:15). Obedience is Jesus's love language!

Scripture Memorization

Psalm 119:30 (ESV) – I have chosen the way of faithfulness; I set your rules before me.

Reflection Questions

1. When you think of loving someone, is obedience one of the first things that comes to mind? If not, what are some of the first things that come to mind when someone is expressing love?

2. Why do you think that showing our love for Jesus is expressed through our obedience?

3. Why do you struggle with disobedience to God?

4. How can obedience to God help a marriage thrive?

ACTIVITY: FINDING OBEDIENCE

Journal prompt: The areas in my life where I could be more obedient to God are...

If we don't know the commands given, how can we ensure that we are being obedient?

Of course, the greatest commandment is love, as we are to love God with all our hearts, minds, and souls. We are also to love our neighbors as we do ourselves. Love is the fulfillment of the Law. If we are acting out love toward each other, we automatically obey the other commandments.

There are many more directives throughout the New Testament. This week choose seven and write them down. Study them throughout the week, perhaps one each day.

If you are eager to know what Jesus says, write them all out!

Pray for obedience to God in all situations

Acts 5:29 I 1 John 5:3 I Isaiah 1:19 I Luke 6:46 I John 14:31

WEEK SEVEN

SHE DOES NOT WORRY

Through reading God's Word, we learn that worry is something we do not have the luxury—or better yet, burden—of doing, because we are to rely on His direction in our lives. He will only lead us to good things, even when it seems that what we are going through is painful. Knowing this, we can honor the decisions He makes for our lives and be okay despite our circumstances. Worry and fear are the opposite of having faith in God.

As human beings, but especially as wives, life takes us on multiple ups and downs. We are often matured into the women we desire to be through trials and tribulations. This is when we must trust God the most. It can be difficult not to worry, but it should not be our go-to when things get rough. What will happen if you or your spouse loses a job or becomes ill? We can't always fall apart when times become difficult. Now granted, we should be gentle with ourselves and give leeway for distressing times, but as mature children of God, we eventually fall back in our Father's arms and our faith in Him. You can't have faith and worry at the same time—you must choose!

Scripture Memorization:

Philippians 4:6–7 (ESV)—Do not be anxious about anything, but in everything by prayer and supplication with thanksgiving let your requests be made known to God. And the peace of God, which surpasses all understanding, will guard your hearts and your minds in Christ Jesus.

Reflection Questions

1. What are some major things you worry about in your life? How can you begin to give them to God and find rest?

2. Imagine your life free from anxiety because you can trust God completely with everything. How would this feel? Describe the feeling.

3. What is the worst-case scenario of possible outcomes of something you currently worry about? Now try to find the bright side of this scenario. Maybe you learn a lesson or grow in patience or faith. Just put a positive spin on whatever it is.

ACTIVITY: TRUST IS A MUST

Journal prompt: *The things I need to give to God and the things I worry about the most are…*

Look up a Scripture on trusting God and write it on several notecards. Keep them in the places you frequent the most— in your office, on the bathroom mirror— and one in your wallet, purse, or pocket.

Every time you are tempted to worry, remember who your Father is, how great He is, and how easily He can turn a situation around in your favor. But we must have faith and trust in Him!

Feel free to use the verses listed below:

Proverbs 3:5–6 — Trust in the Lord with all your heart, and do not lean on your own understanding. In all your ways acknowledge Him, and He will make straight your paths.

Psalm 56:3–4 — When I am afraid, I put my trust in you. In God, whose word I praise, in God I trust; I shall not be afraid. What can flesh do to me?

Psalm 37:5 — Commit your way to the Lord; trust in Him, and He will act.

Isaiah 26:3–4 — You keep him in perfect peace whose mind is stayed on you, because he trusts in You. Trust in the Lord forever, for the Lord God is an everlasting rock.

Psalm 40:4 — Blessed is the man who makes the Lord his trust, who does not turn to the proud, to those who go astray after a lie!

Pray for peace in your heart about anything worrying you

1 Peter 5:7 | Matthew 6:25-34 | Proverbs 12:25 | Matthew 11:28-30 | John 14:27

WEEK EIGHT

SHE HEARS FROM GOD

Before they are spouses or mothers, biblical wives are first and foremost women of God. Their number one priority is God. This includes hearing and following His voice. How can we follow His direction if we are unable to hear His voice? God is always speaking through His Word, so many times it's as simple as opening the Bible and reading about a topic that concerns us. Hearing comes by the word of the Lord, so make sure to stay in your Word even after you have the man.

Scripture Memorization

John 10:27 – My sheep hear my voice, and I know them and they follow me.

Reflection Questions

1. Besides reading the Bible, what are some ways you have heard God speaking to you?

2. Go through the Bible and determine some of the ways people heard from God in the past.

3. How do you think not being able to hear from God will affect your marriage?

ACTIVITY: HEARING HIS VOICE

Journal prompt: *My prayer life can be improved by...*

Make it a point to pray every night this week. After you have prayed, sit quietly for five to ten minutes with a pen and journal and jot down anything that comes to mind.

Pray to hear God's voice

2 Timothy 3:16 I Romans 10:17 I John 8:47 I Revelation 3:20

Monthly Check-in

Did I keep up with my God-plan this month?

Did I hear God's voice this week more than usual?

In what way can I incorporate the practices from the past month into my lifelong term?

Is there anything positive that has occurred as a result of my studies or closer connection with God this month?

TESTIMONY TO SHARE:

Notes

Three

SHE HAS A SERVANT'S HEART

Month Three

She rises while it is still night and gives food to her household and portions to her maidens

Proverbs 31:15

The three women in the following passages were servants in their hearts. The definition of a servant is a person who performs duties for others, a devoted and helpful follower or supporter. As women of God, our hearts should be focused on serving as He leads for His kingdom. Marriage is not for the faint of heart! A marriage is two imperfect people coming together to create a union that (hopefully) God joined together. A godly marriage is full of compromise, give and take and give some more, but it can be a beautiful dance. A good example of a wife who exhibits service is the Proverbs 31 woman. We see that she is described as an extremely unselfish person. Even when she does not feel like serving, many times she still must, as she is committed to her responsibilities as a wife, mother, and entrepreneur.

READINGS

- Genesis 24
- Luke 11:38–42
- Acts 9:36–43

Group Questions

1. Again, we meet Martha. But when reading the passage once more, look at her with new eyes. Notice that her heart is in the right place as she explicitly states that she is a servant. In what ways are you like Martha?

   _____

   _____

   _____

2. Although serving is good to do, it can become a distraction. Why do you think this occurs? How can you ensure your serving of others and the church does not become a hindrance or distraction from your relationship with God?

3. What is the end result of Peter raising Tabitha (Dorcas) from the dead? What does this say about the reason we do God's work?

4. Obviously Tabitha touched a lot of lives through her gifts and was deeply loved. When you picture her, what type of person comes to mind? What does she look like, and what is her demeanor? Do you know any women like this? If you do, make sure you let them know how much they mean to you!

5. What was the result of Rebekah's service? What type of heart did Rebekah have at that time? How can we learn from her actions of service to a stranger?

6. What is your stance on serving your husband? What are some ways that wives get to serve their husbands?

Group Activity: Plan to Serve

Put time aside to serve others this month. Find a place to volunteer, ideally with your Bible study mates as a group.

If you are having problems deciding what to do together, go through the questions below to help decide. Ensure that everyone is included in the decision process and that all voices are heard and respected. Make the choice as a group on a place you all agree on and will feel fulfilled in serving.

To take it further, you can create a list of online databases or websites that connect volunteers with opportunities.

VOLUNTEER QUESTIONNAIRE

What are some things I like to do for fun?	
I feel most fulfilled when I am helping people...	
Is there anything I feel extremely passionate about doing?	
What are some common interests or activities we have as a group?	

Where have people volunteered before? What were their experiences?

Are there any special events coming up that may need volunteers?

What do I hear God saying we should do?

WEEK NINE

SHE SERVES

Jesus came to serve humanity, and if our goal is to look more like Him daily, then service should also be a major role in the life of a Christian. We have received gifts from God, and 1 Peter tells us we are to use them to serve one another as good stewards of God's varied grace. When we reflect on the actions of Martha and Mary, Jesus didn't say that what Martha was doing was bad. On the contrary, it was good. She was just choosing to focus on it at the wrong time. This lets us know we cannot allow service to distract us from our walk with God. A large part of a godly marriage is serving each other and serving God together.

Scripture Memorization

Mark 10:44-45 – And whoever would be first among you must be slave of all. For even the Son of Man came not to be served but to serve, and to give his life as a ransom for many.

Reflection Questions

1. What do you think Jesus meant by "whoever would be first among you must be slave of all"?

2. Look through the Bible and pull out some ways that Jesus served while here on earth.

3. In what ways can you seek to serve those closest to you?

4. What is your feeling on serving your husband? Do you think you would continue to serve him even when you don't want to?

ACTIVITY: A SERVANT'S HEART

Seek to serve those closest to you this week. If you live with others, help more around the house or make it a point to ask if you can serve in some way. If you live alone, you can seek to serve at your job, maybe clean the fridge if it hasn't been done in a while, or ask around to see if anyone needs assistance. Just commit to being more helpful. Don't forget to log your activity!

Journal prompt: *I honestly don't feel like serving when…*

THIS WEEK I SERVED OTHERS BY:

Monday	
Tuesday	
Wednesday	
Thursday	
Friday	
Saturday	
Sunday	

Pray for discernment about how and where you should serve more

Ephesians 6:7 I Galatians 5:13 I 1 Peter 4:11 I Mark 9:35

WEEK TEN

SHE GIVES TO THE NEEDY

Second Corinthians 8:9 tells us that Jesus was rich and became poor for us to become rich. What a great example of selflessness and giving to those in need. The Bible tells us that whoever is generous to the poor lends to the Lord and that *He* will repay them for their deed. Giving to others, especially the needy, is an important part of our walk as Christian women and wives.

Scripture Memorization

Proverbs 19:17 — Whoever is generous to the poor lends to the Lord.

Reflection Questions

1. The Scripture states that when we lend to the poor, we lend to the Lord. What else does the Bible say about the poor?

2. How can you seek to be more generous to the poor?

3. Why do you think it is important to not do your good acts before others? (Matthew 6:1-4)

4. Can you imagine ways you and your husband can give to the needy together?

ACTIVITY: PAY IT FORWARD

Journal prompt: When I see a poor person on the street, I feel...

There will always be someone less fortunate than you. From doing something as simple as paying for someone's coffee, gas, or groceries to volunteering at a shelter, this week commit to helping others, by paying it forward through simple acts of kindness, especially those in need.

WAYS THAT I PAID IT FORWARD THIS WEEK!

DATE	HOW I PAID IT FORWARD	HOW I FELT AFTER

Pray to have a heart that sees opportunity to help those less fortunate

Leviticus 25:35 I Proverbs 28:27 I Luke 12:33–34 I Proverbs 19:17

WEEK ELEVEN

SHE IS UNSELFISH

Our ultimate example of giving is Jesus Christ—He gave His life to save ours. Nothing we do or give could repay what He did for us. He gave without expecting anything in return, except that we be grateful for His sacrifice. Sacrificial giving can often be painful, but it's worth it. When we give, we should do so with an open heart and let go of expectations of returns. We should give cheerfully as we learn that the Lord loves a cheerful giver (2 Corinthians 9:7). It is more blessed to give than to receive (Acts 20:35), and we give out of love and a heart that seeks the best for others.

Scripture Memorization

Luke 6:38 (NASB) — Give, and it will be given to you. They will pour into your lap a good measure – pressed down, shaken together, and running over. For by your standard of measure it will be measured to you in return.

Reflection Questions

1. What does it mean that what we are given is to be pressed down, shaken together, and running over?

2. How would you rate yourself on the scale of being a giver?
    a. I'm not giving anything unless I'm getting something out of the deal.
    b. Stingy, but I'll give a little and expect others to give back; I get upset and feel like I'm being taken advantage of if they don't.
    c. I give and take about equally.
    d. I give a lot compared to some.
    e. I love to give to others and see them happy; I don't notice or expect anything in return.

3. How can being stingy in a marriage wreak havoc in the relationship? Why do you think it's important to become a cheerful giver prior to marriage?

4. How do you find the line between being a giver and being a doormat?

ACTIVITY: THE GIFT OF GIVING

Journal prompt: I find myself being most selfish when…

Go out of your way to give this week! Make a list of people who you can give to each day of the week, and walk it out. It could be giving your time by going to see your grandmother who is always asking you to visit, or leaving a present for a coworker who's been down. No matter how big or small, make it a point to do something thoughtful every day for someone else without expectation of return. You don't even have to let them know who did it.

If you feel the Holy Spirit moving you to give sacrificially then do so. This is giving like Jesus. Give something you are having a hard time letting go of. It could be a large amount of money or a favorite dress you adore. Pray and listen intently this week to hear if God is wanting you to give something more while keeping in mind that obedience is greater than sacrifice in God's eyes (1 Samuel 15:22)

Monday	
Tuesday	
Wednesday	
Thursday	
Friday	
Saturday	
Sunday	

Pray for an unselfish heart

Hebrews 13:16 | 2 Corinthians 9:7 | Philippians 2:4 | 2 Timothy 3:2–4

WEEK TWELVE

SHE MINISTERS

We have established that a godly wife and woman is one who is after God's own heart. Besides serving in the wife and mother ministries, a godly wife often serves in ministry at her church. Although service in the church should never come before your relationship and walk with God, ministries and ministering to people in these outreaches should be a major part of our fellowship with others. We are instructed to not forsake the gathering together and to encourage each other—ministry is a great way to do this!

Scripture Memorization

Hebrews 10:24–25 (NASB) — And let us consider how to stimulate one another to love and good deeds, not forsaking our own assembling together, as is the habit of some, but encouraging one another; and all the more as you see the day drawing near.

Reflection Questions

1. Why do you feel that Jesus told you it is more blessed to give than to receive?

2. What day is this verse speaking of in Hebrews 10:25? Why is it capitalized in some texts?

3. How will you ensure to prevent church-ministry burnout?

ACTIVITY: MINSTERIAL ACTS

Journal prompt: *I feel fulfilled in ministry when…*

If you aren't already serving in some capacity at a church, then think of a way to get more involved in ministry. No matter how big or small the church, I am sure there is always a need. Make a concerted effort to at least do one thing this week to get you started. It can be as simple as obtaining a list of ministries, or speaking to your pastor about where the need is greatest.

If you are just bogged down and can't commit to anything now, perhaps they have on-call or special events positions. But don't overload yourself; we can even get too involved with church duties and neglect God Himself.

Pray for God to reveal where you should serve in ministry

Ephesians 4:11–13 I 2 Timothy 2:15 I 2 Corinthians 6:3–10 I 2 Corinthians 4:1–2

Monthly Check-in

Did I keep up with my God-plan this month?

How do I improve for next month?

What is my strategy for becoming a woman after God's own heart?

Is there anything positive that has occurred as a result of my studies or closer connection with God this month?

TESTIMONY TO SHARE:

Notes

Four

SHE IS STRONG

Month Four

She girds herself with strength and makes her arms strong

Proverbs 31:17

We meet strong women throughout the Bible and in life. In fact, as godly wives we become strong women through being overcomers and preservers. Take the time to really delve into the reading and search out the qualities and characteristics that made these women strong women of God.

READING

- Judges 4

Group Questions

1. When you meet Deborah and Jael in the passage, what comes to mind about the type of women they may be? How do they both exhibit varying types of strength?

   _____
   _____
   _____
   _____
   _____

2. Deborah is a woman that stands out in the Bible for many reasons. One big reason is her high-profile position as a judge. She is the only female judge mentioned in the Bible and she seems to be well respected by her peers. Do you believe she was fearful of doing some of the things God called her to?

   _____
   _____
   _____
   _____

3. Many times when God calls us to do things, they aren't easy and may bring up some trepidation about moving forward. What things is God calling you to do that may scare you or make you fearful? How can you work through this to follow God's plan for your life?

   _____
   _____
   _____
   _____
   _____

4. Why do you think Barak would not do what God told him to unless Deborah went with them? What was the consequence of this action?

   _____
   _____
   _____

5. As a prophetess, wife, and judge, Deborah juggled many duties. What do you envision her prayer life and walk with God to be?

   _____
   _____
   _____
   _____

6. The term *milk and honey* is used in the Bible to denote abundance and to describe parts of the promise land. Sisera asks for water when he makes it into Jael's tent, but she gave him milk. Can you speculate why she may have done so?

   _____
   _____
   _____

7. Can you think of and share a story where you had to have a tremendous amount of faith?

   _____
   _____

_____

_____

8. Can you think of and share cases where you have seen a tremendous amount of faith required in a marriage?

_____

_____

_____

_____

Group Activity: Overcomer

Many times, the hardest tests in our lives teach us the biggest lessons.

Think of at least three trials in your life. Write them down on the left hand of the page. Now think of how this made you a stronger woman and some of the lessons you learned from them. Share at least one to encourage your group.

Test or Trial

Lesson Learned

To take it further: Is there a way for you to share your lessons learned with others? Can you start a blog, write a post on social media, or simply encourage someone else with your wisdom?

Test or Trial	Lesson Learned
Test or Trial	Lesson Learned
Test or Trial	Lesson Learned

See how strong you are!

WEEK THIRTEEN

SHE HAS STRONG MENTAL FORTITUDE

Although our Scripture readings for this month portray a very brutal strength in Deborah and Jael, our strength will most likely be exhibited in other ways. Through the story we do see one quality that carries through to us today—possessing a very strong mental fortitude. As Christians, this comes from having a deep faith in God that has been developed over time through tests and trials and relying on His supernatural power and grace in times of need. A strong woman of God is well aware of where her strength comes from.

Scripture Memorization

Romans 5:3-4 – Not only that, but we rejoice in our sufferings, knowing that suffering produces endurance, and endurance produces character, and character produces hope

Reflection Questions

1. How do you get from suffering to hope when you go through trials?

2. Read Romans 5:5. Why do you think hope will not put us to shame? What exactly does this mean?

3. Determine where you find yourself when trials, hardships and tribulations come. Do you usually fall apart? Do you always call someone else to bail you out? Do you take your frustrations out on others? Think about how you have handled trials in the past and how you can improve upon this the next time.

ACTIVITY: COUNTING IT ALL JOY

Journal prompt: *I feel empowered and disempowered most when...*

Granted, when we receive bad news or go through some sort of test or trial, our first instinct may be to act out, become depressed or take out our frustration on someone else. But that isn't the way that God says we are to handle the stresses that come with everyday life. We are supposed to count it all joy (James 1:2). Marriage is full of ups and downs, and for your union to have longevity, you will go through things together where you will have to hold strong to this Scripture.

This week, practice counting it all joy. When you come into a trial, no matter how small, attempt to see the good or lesson in what you are going through. If you can't see the good or any lesson, then praise God through it anyway because you know that everything is working according to His plan and will work out in your favor regardless of your limited vision.

Pray for increased faith when tests and trials come your way

Revelation 21:8 I 2 Timothy 1:7 I Ephesians 6:10 I Philippians 4:13

WEEK FOURTEEN

SHE HAS A QUIET, GENTLE, PEACEFUL SPIRIT

When we read 1 Peter 3:4–6, we find that having a gentle and quiet spirit comes from adorning yourself through submission to your husband and having faith in God. Meaning, we should be more concerned with what we are putting on the inside of us than the outside. No two women are alike—there are loud and boisterous women as well as quiet and shy women—but this is an outward expression. All women can still possess quiet, peaceful, and gentle spirits through following the directives of the Lord.

Scripture Memorization

1 Peter 3:4— but let your adorning be the hidden person of the heart with the imperishable beauty of a gentle and quite spirit, which in God's sight is very precious

Reflection Questions

1. Why do you think having a gentle and quiet spirit is of great worth in God's eyes?

2. What does it mean to have a gentle and quiet spirit? What does that look like to you? What does the opposite look like?

3. How do you think having a quiet and peaceful spirit in marriage is beneficial?

ACTIVITY: SPIRIT SCALES

Journal prompt: *My spirit is most at peace when…*

The world often shows strength as being manipulative, seductive, or vengeful. But a strong woman of God is quite the opposite. She is kind, compassionate, and considerate in the face of worldly trials. Make a chart of what the world says versus what God says about being a strong woman using the chart below. Then each day monitor your interactions with others, to determine where you might fall on the scale. We all have our off days, and no one is perfect; so if you find yourself showing strength the world's way, don't beat yourself up about it. The important thing is that you have the desire and will to shift to doing things God's way!

GOD'S WAY	THE WORLD'S WAY

Pray for a spirit pleasing to God

Colossians 3:12 I Matthew 11:29 I 1 Peter 3:15 I Proverbs 15:1

WEEK FIFTEEN

SHE IS DISCIPLINED

Journal prompt: I need more discipline in the area of...

The definition of self-discipline is the ability to control one's feelings and overcome weaknesses, the ability to pursue what one thinks is right despite temptations to abandon it. Being self-disciplined can take a great deal of tenacity, especially when you may not want to do certain things. Dealing with life can sometimes get to be a struggle, and the fact that we have our flesh pulling us to do what it wants makes it even more difficult. Learn what the Bible says about self-discipline and the flesh so you will have the tools to put it into submission.

Scripture Memorization

1 Corinthians 9:27 – But I discipline my body and keep it under control, lest after preaching to other I myself should be disqualified.

Reflection Questions

1. How do you ensure that you are not being controlled by your flesh now?

2. What are some areas where you can improve your self-control prior to marriage (e.g., finances, overspending, budgeting, holding your tongue, listening, completing a project or a book)?

3. What are the major differences between self-discipline and self-control?

4. What are some things more prone to happening in a marriage when neither party is disciplined or controlled by their flesh?

ACTIVITY: NO EXCUSES

Take one thing from your list in question 2 and purpose to be disciplined in this area.

If your thing was finishing a book, purpose to sit down a little bit each day this week to write in it, even if just for ten minutes a day. If it is overspending, have the discipline to stick to a budget and not make impulse purchases. Make no excuses for your flesh and strive to remain disciplined. Write about your experience below.

MY ONE THING: _____

MONDAY	
TUESDAY	
WEDNESDAY	
THURSDAY	
FRIDAY	
SATURDAY	
SUNDAY	

Pray for the strength of self-control, especially in an area where you

Romans 8:5 I Titus 1:7–8 I 2 Peter 1:4–6 I Hebrews 12:11

WEEK SIXTEEN

SHE IS SUBMISSIVE

Submission to some of us is like a foul word! But God tells us it is a good thing for each to do to the other. Long before a godly wife is submissive to a husband, she has practiced and mastered submitting to her heavenly covering, God. Submission is necessary for your walk with God and, per the Bible, your walk with your husband. It takes real strength to submit to another's will when you want to do things your way.

We are told in the Bible that a wife is to submit to her husband. This in no way means that you are a doormat, subservient or less than, but we do have our God-given roles in a marriage. We are all submissive to someone at some point in time; as children we were submissive to our parents, and as adults many of us submit to our bosses. Take some time to read about and learn what God thinks of submission this week.

Scripture Memorization

James 4:7 – Submit yourselves therefore to God. Resist the devil, and he will flee from you.

Reflection Questions

1. How do you honestly feel about submission? Is it like a foul word to you, or do you not have an issue with it? Why or why not?

2. Can you think of any examples of submission in the Bible?

3. Why do you think God stated that a wife is to submit to her husband?

4. How can submission be a good thing in a marriage—both to each other, and a wife to her husband?

ACTIVITY: LEARNING SUBMISSION

Journal prompt: When God tells me to do something I don't want to, I feel...

Think of something you have not been submissive to God's will in and put forth in doing it this week. It could be having a difficult conversation you didn't want to have, forgiving someone, breaking off an unhealthy relationship, or simply spending more alone time with Him.

Also take the time to discuss submission with some wise married women you know. Write below what they tell you and discuss with your Bible study group at your next meeting.

Answer the questions below:

What did you learn in the activity this week?

What did you accomplish?

What was the most difficult part of the activity this week?

Pray for submission to God's will

Ephesians 5:21 | Ephesians 5:22–24 | Luke 22:42 | 1 Peter 3:5–6

Monthly Check-in

Did I keep up with my God-plan this month?

Are there still areas where I can be more disciplined in life?

I still need to work on _____

Is there anything positive that has occurred as a result of my studies or closer connection with God this month?

TESTIMONY TO SHARE:

Notes

Five

SHE ESTABLISHES HER TEMPLE

Month Five

Strength and dignity are her clothing, and she smiles at the future.

Proverbs 31:25

A strong godly woman is confident and knows what she brings to the table. She is able to realize this because of her relationship with herself and God. She understands that she is a prize and very much a blessing to her husband and family. Two of the most important relationships you have in life are with yourself and God. If you aren't happy with those, then it is highly unlikely you'll be happy in a relationship. You desire a love that lasts a lifetime after the wedding day, so concentrating on getting these relationships on track is critical to a healthy, mutually beneficial relationship.

READING

- John 4:1–45

Group Questions

1. Look at the way the Samaritan woman thought of herself (v. 9) and how the disciples thought of her (v. 27). Do you think she had high or low self-esteem? Which well was she drawing her self-esteem from?

   _____
   _____
   _____

2. Compare the way Jesus treats the woman at the well with how she herself and society expected Him to treat her. What are the major differences that you can surmise?

   _____
   _____
   _____
   _____

3. Are there things about yourself that cause you a lack of confidence, possibly things that the world may not deem attractive or acceptable? Are there times when you are afraid that God will reject you because of these things?

   _____
   _____
   _____
   _____
   _____

4. God sees all and knows what goes on in our lives. We all have thoughts or actions we aren't so proud of, but what can you learn about conviction from the Samaritan woman's reaction? How can you apply this teaching to your own life?

   _____
   _____
   _____
   _____

5. What was the result of the Samaritan woman sharing her testimony with others?

   _____
   _____

6. Reread verses 35–38. Here Jesus is speaking of reaping and sowing. We are able to receive the ultimate harvest because Jesus sowed seeds of life on our behalf. Think of your future children and grandchildren. What are you sowing for them now? What negative mindsets are you holding on to that need to be released so they won't be instilled in future generations?

   _____
   _____
   _____
   _____
   _____

Group Activity: Testimony Time

Use the space below to write a paragraph or two about a particular testimony or your testimony in general. Take an allotted amount of time to share your testimony with your study group.

To take it further: Think of someone else that this testimony could help if they heard it, and share it with them. It could be a friend, a church member, another study group, or if you have a larger platform such as social media or blog, share it there. You never know how you could help someone else and bring them into the belief of God and how great He is!

My Testimony

_____
_____
_____
_____
_____
_____
_____
_____
_____
_____
_____
_____

Whom else can I share my testimony with?

WEEK SEVENTEEN

SHE KNOWS HER WORTH

When a godly man who already has the mentality of taking on the role of a husband meets you, he has found his good thing, and the Lord favors him! Wives bring so much into a God-given husband's life, including blessings from above. He receives favor because he has found you, a woman who is already a wife, because you have prepared your heart and mind. You must realize and know your worth because, per God himself, you are the prize!

Scripture Memorization

Proverbs 18:22 — He who finds a wife finds a good thing and obtains favor from the Lord.

Reflection Questions

1. Have there been times in your life where you played a role less than that given to you by God? Where did you fall short?

2. Do you believe that the man should seek out and approach the woman, or is it open for either to approach the other?

3. Why do you think God made the wife of a godly husband such a blessing to his life?

4. How do you become a wife even before obtaining a ring?

Journal prompt: *I know I am awesome because…*

ACTIVITY: PRECIOUS PRIZES

This week, give thought to how you may be selling yourself short in relationships with men or how you have in the past.

How can you ensure that you always think of and carry yourself as the prize?

Look at the supplemental verses and see what else you can find about how you will benefit your God-given husband. You can use the space below to record your findings.

Pray for God to reveal how precious you are in His eyes.

Proverbs 12:4 | Proverbs 19:14 | Proverbs 31:10 | 1 Peter 3:7

WEEK EIGHTEEN

SHE HAS DEALT WITH PAST ISSUES

When we hold on to things that happened in the past, we ultimately drag them into the future. Don't allow your past to make you bitter but allow the lessons you learned to make you better. If you still feel frustrated or angry thinking about an ex or someone who wronged you, then you are still holding on to bitterness and frustration. Don't allow these feelings to take up any more room in your heart. Leave them where they are so they don't travel into the future with you.

Scripture Memorization

Ephesians 4:31 — Let all bitterness and wrath and anger and clamor and slander be put away from you, along with all malice.

Psalm 147:3 — He heals the brokenhearted and binds up their wounds.

Reflection Questions

1. Read 2 Corinthians 1:4, 8–10. What are some reasons we go through heartache, trials, and tests?

2. What is one thing you still must let go of in your heart? Why do you think it's still there? How does it serve you? (For example, do you gain sympathy from others when you bring it up? Does it keep up your wall so you won't get hurt again?)

3. What does the Bible say about bitterness and anger?

4. How do you think holding on to past pains and frustrations could affect a new relationship?

ACTIVITY: LETTING GO!

Journal prompt: *Letting go of past hurts and pains feels…*

Use the drawings of suitcases on the next page to write things you are carrying over from a previous relationship, something from a family member, friend, or even bullies from school. Write down anything you are having a hard time letting go of because of something someone did or said to you. Make sure you label who it is from, then cut them out and let it go!

Also, create a master plan as to how you will begin unpacking, and do at least one thing on that list this week (e.g., speaking to a trained counselor or apologizing to someone). Write at least three things below; if you get to all three this week, great!

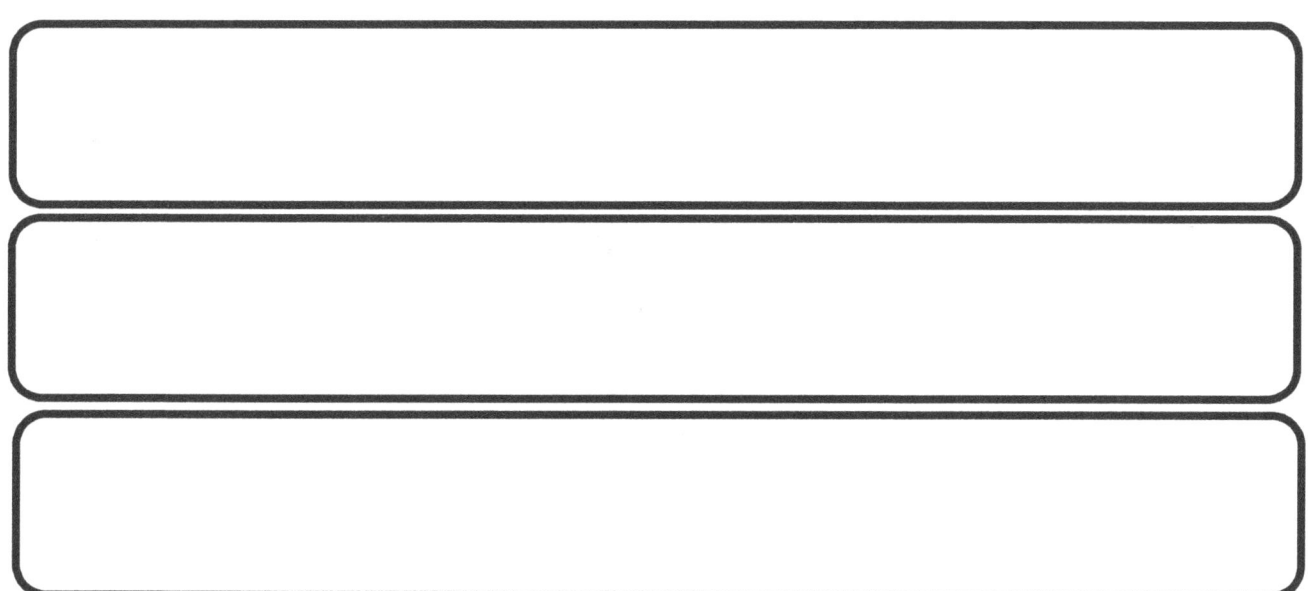

Pray for help to release anything you are holding on to from the past

2 Corinthians 7:9 I 2 Corinthians 1:4; 1:8-10 I Ephesians 4:21–24

SUITCASES

SUITCASES

WEEK NINETEEN

SHE IS GENTLE WITH HERSELF

Your inner-self relationship and talk is critical to the way you view yourself, others, and the world. Having positive self-dialogue and thoughts are a necessary fundamental in building healthy relationships. If you are constantly criticizing yourself and others in your head, it comes across in your energy. Your internal relationship with yourself is an extremely important one; in fact, it is the most important relationship here on earth. Take some time to read about what the Bible says about you and confess it over your life this week!

Scripture Memorization

Philippians 4:8 — Finally, brothers, whatever is true, whatever is honorable, whatever is just, whatever is pure, whatever is lovely, whatever is commendable, if there is any excellence, if there is anything worthy of praise, think about these things.

Reflection Questions

1. Why do you think it's so important to have a joyful heart?

2. What things does Jesus say about joy?

3. The Bible tells us to love each other as we love ourselves. What does love look like if you aren't first loving yourself?

4. How do you think having a negative self-dialogue can impact yourself and your marriage?

ACTIVITY: BE CAREFUL WITH YOU

Journal prompt: *If my friend talked to me the way I talk to myself in my head, I would…*

This week, practice being positive no matter what! Have you ever seen a movie where there is this chipper, always happy, always-looking-on-the-bright-side character who constantly has a smile on their face? Well, think of this challenge as that person living inside your mind. No matter what happens, refuse to look on the negative side of a situation, and choose to see the bright side.

Write down your experiences and thoughts this week.

Pray to always see the best in yourself.

Proverbs 17:22 | Matthew 15:11 | Romans 12:2 | Proverbs 18:21

WEEK TWENTY

SHE HAS HEALTHY PRACTICES

Jesus came to heal the sick and commanded His disciples to do the same (Matthew 10:8). We all have something that needs healing. It is important to have both mental and physical healthy practices, so if there is something health wise concerning you, take care of it now. Healthy practices include mental, spiritual, and physical. Many of the activities this month may be long-term activities and are some that you may want to incorporate into your daily life, so don't just do them for a week and forget—continue the ones you find most helpful! Remember, if you don't do the work and do it consistently, your dream will most likely remain a dream.

Scripture Memorization

1 Peter 2:24 — He himself bore our sins in his body on the tree, that we might die to sin and live to righteousness. By his wounds you have been healed.

Reflection Questions

1. Why do you think Jesus loved us enough to die for us?

2. Jesus healed many people, and in some cases, He asked them, "What do you want me to do for you?" or "Do you want to be healed?" If Jesus asked you these questions, how would you respond?

3. Husbands are called to love their wives as Jesus loved the church. What does this mean, and what does it look like to you?

ACTIVITY: ASSESSING LIFE

Journal prompt: *I can do better health wise with...*

Health assessment challenge — what does perfect, optimal health look like to you in each of these areas? What do you have to do to get there?

	VISION	PLAN	STEPS
MENTAL			
PHYSICAL			
SPIRITUAL			

Pray for good health both mentally and physically

3 John 1:2 | 1 Corinthians 6:19–20 | Proverbs 3:7–8; 4:20–22 | 1 Timothy 4:8

Monthly Check-in

Did I keep up with my God-plan this month?

What will I continue from this month's activities?

How will I begin to hold myself accountable for the time I spend with God and moving toward the direction He desires for my life?

Is there anything positive that has occurred as a result of my studies or closer connection with God this month?

TESTIMONY TO SHARE:

Notes

Six

SHE BUILDS HER HOUSE

Month Six

She is not afraid of snow for her household, for all her household are

Proverbs 31:21

Throughout the Bible we see examples of women building and keeping their homes, both physically and metaphorically. These examples are shown through their honoring God, providing and accepting guidance, caring for those in their home and being encouragers. The following reading is a well-known and highly reviewed story that is an awesome example of a woman who builds her home.

READING

- The book of Ruth

Group Questions

1. In this passage we read about three main women: Naomi, Ruth, and Orpah. Ruth was a Moabite woman, and the Moabites were known to worship other gods, particularly Chemosh. There is no doubt Orpah and Ruth both loved Naomi and it was difficult to leave her, but what are the major differences you see when you compare Orpah's and Ruth's loyalty to Naomi—and, most importantly, to God?

   _____
   _____
   _____
   _____
   _____
   _____

2. In the book of Ruth, we see that Naomi probably had a plan or vision for Ruth's future. How is this depicted throughout the book?

   _____
   _____

3. We see Ruth caring for Naomi as she works in the field and encourages her through a rough time for both of them. What can you take away from this attitude that you can apply to your own life?

4. How does Boaz describe Ruth?

5. In verses 13 through 22, we see another example of choices made that will affect future generations. Can you identify some choices made by your mother or grandmother that either led to positive generational legacies or negative ones?

6. Describe Ruth's interactions with Boaz: how does she treat him, speak to him, honor him?

Group Activity: Ask, Believe, Receive

Do you think that Ruth had goals for her life? If so, do you think they were all fulfilled. My guess would be probably not, but that's because God had better for her life. She became part of the Jesus' blood line by not following her own ambitions but those of God.

This month have a God & Goals party! Create some goals for your life 1, 2 & 5 years from now. Also include some God sized goals, like paying off a ton of debt in a short amount of time or getting to go on that dream trip you didn't think was possible next year. Include the areas of finances, spiritual growth, relationships, career and fitness.

Keep in mind that you are asking the Father if you can have these things in this life, but if He sees fit that they don't come about, then be okay with that because ultimately it is for our best interest and our protection. The Bible does tell us to ask, believe, and receive, but we must not ask amiss.

Seek God on what you should place on your goal chart, and if it's a no, leave it off. We always want to be aligned with His will.

Make sure to pray as a group before starting your God & Goals Party. Pray to remain focused on God's desires for your life as well as against idol worship of your visions, dreams, and goals.

Discuss year one and God goals in your group.

Take it further: Place Scripture on your goal chart! Here are some suggestions:

Job 1:21, Luke 22:42, Romans 12:2

1 year

2 years

5 years

God Goals

WEEK TWENTY-ONE

SHE IS AN ENCOURAGER

A godly wife is one who builds her family up, and one way she does this is by using words of encouragement. As women, we are able to encourage growth and success in our husbands, children, and those around us. If wielded correctly, our words can produce powerful, positive results! Proverbs 14:1 states that a wise woman builds her house, but the foolish one tears hers down with her own hands. We must determine what type of wife we are going to be—one who builds or one who destroys.

Scripture Memorization

Ephesians 4:29 — *Let no corrupt talk come out of your mouths, but only such as is good for building up, as fits the occasion, that it may give grace to those who hear.*

Reflection Questions

1. Can you think of an instance in your past relationships where you have torn your partner down? How do you think this made him feel? What could you have done different in that instance?

2. Read Proverbs 21:9, 19; 27:15; and 25:24. Do you think the husbands of wives with this character feel blessed? What type of marriage do you envision?

3. Husbands need lots of encouragement, even in the small things. How is encouragement and focusing on the positives of a person much better than focusing on the negatives or nagging?

ACTIVITY: THE GREAT ENCOURAGER

Journal prompt: When someone encourages me, I feel...

Try to be encouraging this week—to friends, coworkers, and family. Find ways to be genuinely encouraging and complimentary.

Being an encourager means getting outside of yourself and taking note of what other people are doing and expressing genuine interest and cheering them on in their accomplishments. Truly take the time to invest in others this week.

Make a list of times you've been an encourager. How did you feel, and what did you learn? Share it with your study group.

Pray for God's guidance in encouraging others.

1 Thessalonians 5:11 I Romans 15:4 I 1 Thessalonians 4:15–18 I Proverbs 16:24

WEEK TWENTY-TWO

SHE IS THE KEEPER OF HER HOME

The Proverbs 31 woman was a woman who without a doubt knew the importance of taking care of home. A woman's priority in a home is to set the tone or vibe. Will your home be one of peace and rest or turmoil and arguments? Like a beautiful woman with a horrible attitude, a home can be decorated beautifully and the landscape flawless, but if the atmosphere on the inside is one of strife and negativity, it isn't a home many people would want to live in.

Scripture Memorization

Isaiah 32:18 — My people will abide in a peaceful habitation, in secure dwellings, and in quiet resting places.

Reflection Questions

1. What do you think the Proverbs 31 woman's house looked like on the inside?

2. What are some ways you can create a peaceful, spirit-filled atmosphere in your home?

3. Do you feel differently when there is clutter surrounding you than when your home is clean and orderly?

4. Why is it so important to be a keeper of peace in your home?

ACTIVITY: HOUSE OR HOME

Journal prompt: I think gender roles are...

Challenge yourself to take care of home this week.

Get to that task around the house you have been putting off. First identify it, and then make a to-do list as to how you are going to accomplish the task.

It may be organizing that closet or junk drawer, or it may simply just be tidying up and keeping things in their proper places.

What did you accomplish this week?

Pray for a holy home

Titus 2:5 I Proverbs 14:14 I 1 Samuel 25:6 I Proverbs 3:33

WEEK TWENTY-THREE

SHE HAS VISION

A wise woman has a vision for her household and family, even before they come to pass. She knows the importance of building a house on a good, solid foundation. She also recognizes that these things may not come about in the way she expects. She has learned to be okay with God's plans. There is nothing wrong with making plans and having vision, but there is something wrong with holding on too tightly to the outcome or the way these things happen. Even with your vision, you must keep in mind that you aren't the only one in the relationship, so things may not go according to your plan. Keep in mind that Jesus is ultimately in control.

Scripture Memorization

Proverbs 14:1 — The wisest of women builds her house, but folly with her own hands tears it down.

Reflection Questions

1. Compare and contrast the wise versus the foolish woman. How does one build and one tear down?

2. Would you say that in your past relationships you played the role of a wise woman or a foolish woman?

3. If you think of this verse as it is speaking of relationships, what can you do now to ensure you are a wise woman when you get married?

ACTIVITY: LIFE MISSION

Journal prompt: *If my vision marriage does not go as planned, I will be...*

Having a life mission statement is a smart way to keep your ultimate long-term life goals in focus. This week, write a mission for your own life. What is your vision for your life?

Look up sample mission statements. Here are some details about mission statements to help you get started:

- They are usually short, about one paragraph.
- Your life mission statement should detail your life purpose and direction.
- It should answer the question, What do you value as an individual and couple?
- What are your desires and intents? What matters to you?

> **MY LIFE MISSION STATEMENT**

Pray to be aligned with God's vision for your future.

Proverbs 16:9 | Jeremiah 29:11 | Psalm 119:105 | Proverbs 19:21

WEEK TWENTY-FOUR

SHE KNOWS WHOSE SHE IS

A mature, wise woman knows who and whose she is. She has taken the time to learn her likes and dislikes, to discover and work on her flaws. She has learned to love herself as a human being regardless of what those around her say. She is a woman who has overcome people bondage and has broken the chains of living for anyone else but herself and God. This week, find Scripture that focuses on becoming a woman who knows who and whose she is.

Scripture Memorization

Psalm 139:23 – Search me, O God, and know my heart! Try me and know my thoughts!

Reflection Questions

1. Are there things that keep you in people bondage? Are there times when you find yourself not doing what God would want because you want to fit in or are afraid of what others will say or think about you?

2. In the story of Ruth, we see that although Ruth was born into another tribe, she knew who she belonged with. She wasn't concerned about what her family back home would say or think because she chose to follow God's people. How can we begin to know and live life only for God's approval?

3. How can not knowing yourself or who you are prior to marriage be detrimental?

ACTIVITY: KNOW THYSELF

Journal prompt: I still feel insecure when ...

This week focus on where you still feel the pull of people bondage. Decide that you will walk like Ruth in all you do and seek to follow God's desires.

Below, write out ten things you know about yourself.

1.
2.
3.
4.
5.
6.
7.
8.
9.
10.

Pray for the courage to always choose God.

Galatians 1:10 I John 12:43 I Psalm 118:6–9 I 1 Thessalonians 2:4

Monthly Check-in

Did I keep up with my God-plan this month?

What did I discover about myself this month?

How can I ensure that I remain focused on my life's mission?

Is there anything positive that has occurred as a result of my studies or closer connection with God this month?

TESTIMONY TO SHARE:

Notes

Seven

SHE BRINGS HER HUSBAND GOOD

Month Seven

The heart of her husband trusts in her, and he will have no lack of gain. She does him good and not evil all the days of her life.

Proverbs 31:11-12

There are many passages throughout the Bible about how a husband and wife should treat each other. We find that wives should be respectful, accepting, and peaceable, among other things. In this passage, we read about a woman who brought her husband good unbeknownst to him and possibly undeservingly.

READING

- 1 Samuel 25

Group Questions

1. 1 Samuel 25:3 tells us that Abigail had beauty and brains, but her husband's name literally means "fool"! Compare and contrast some of the other qualities you see in each of them throughout the reading.

   _____
   _____
   _____
   _____

2. Nabal's response was going to bring death and destruction to his own people. David was on his way to kill Nabal while he was drunk and partying, unaware of what was to come—all because of his poor response! Words have such power! In what ways can you choose your words more carefully going forward?

   _____
   _____

3. David made sure to tell his servants to greet Nabal cordially, but they were met with a surly and less than respectful response. Place yourself on both sides of the coin—being asked to do something you don't want to do and being rejected or denied something you really wanted or felt you deserved. What is your usual response in each situation? Would your response be closest to a Nabal, Abigail, or David?

_____
_____
_____

4. Abigail had studied her husband and knew when not to bother him with the details. She used good judgment in her approach to Nabal. Why is this an excellent quality for a wife to have?

_____
_____
_____

5. What can you learn from this Bible passage about marriage, specifically, covering and loving your husband even when he isn't acting lovable or deserving?

_____
_____
_____

6. In the end God avenged David through the death of Nabal. What does this tell us about God?

_____
_____
_____

Group Activity: What I like about ME!

Make a list of at least ten things you like about yourself and that you feel would bring your husband good. If you're ambitious, try for one hundred throughout this month!

1.

2.

3.

4.

5.

6.

7.

8.

9.

10.

WEEK TWENTY-FIVE

SHE IS TRUSTWORTHY

Not only is a godly wife a woman after God's own heart, she is one that seeks the heart of her husband. She does so through proving to be a trustworthy spouse. This means she is very forthcoming and honest and not manipulative. This also means he can trust her to make wise, discerning decisions. He knows he can come to her with issues and dilemmas and trust her wise council. He trusts that she is consistently speaking to and hearing from God as both a woman of God and a godly wife.

Scripture Memorization

Proverbs 12:22 – Lying lips are an abomination to the Lord, but those who act faithfully are his delight.

Reflection Questions

1. The Lord hates a lying tongue. Why do you think it is such a vile act to Him?

2. What are some ways you have manipulated a significant other? What was the result? Did you wind up getting what you wanted?

3. What are some ways you can be more truthful, even with "little white lies"?

4. Besides the ways listed above, what are some ways you show your trustworthiness in a relationship with your significant other?

ACTIVITY: IN THE EAVES

Journal prompt: When someone lies to me or attempts to manipulate me, I feel ...

Imagine you are in the next room and can hear your significant other's conversation. He is talking to his mom about you and how much you have blessed his life. How do you want him to describe you (e.g., she cooks well, she pampers me, she's a great mom, she's in great shape, she is so kind and patient)? The sky's the limit, but come up with at least ten attributes you want to bless your husband with.

Take the statements from the dream activity for this month that you want to bless your husband with and turn them into affirmations. For example, if you overheard your husband say you were an awesome cook, your statement may be something like "I am an awesome cook" or "I am becoming a great cook for my family." Repeat these affirmations to yourself daily this week.

Pray for an honest and pure heart and for conviction when it is not.

Proverbs 19:1 I John 8:32 I Proverbs 11:3 I Colossians 3:9

1.

2.

3.

4.

5.

6.

7.

8.

9.

10.

WEEK TWENTY-SIX

SHE IS IN CONTROL OF HER EMOTIONS & TONGUE

When we think of a godly wife, the first thing that comes to mind is not a screaming hothead who has little to no control over her emotions or tongue. Throughout the Bible, women of God are humble, generous with their kind words, and self-controlled. A godly wife is not constantly nagging, talking down to, or disrespecting her husband. She can keep her emotions in check and use them as indicators, not dictators, because she values her position as a woman of God and her family. She recognizes the benefit of not allowing her moods to run her.

As wives, we will have opportunities to say or do mean things, but that is where self-control comes in. Think of your flesh like a five-year-old who constantly wants what she wants, and when she doesn't get it, she flies off the handle, throws temper tantrums, yells, screams, and throws things. If you let your flesh run your life and emotions, it's akin to a five-year-old running them! The ability to control oneself, particularly your emotions and tongue, is a sign of maturity. Godly wives are mature enough to realize that gaining control over their flesh and tongue prior to marriage gives them a great advantage going into a union.

Scripture Memorization

Proverbs 25:28 –A man without self-control is like a city broken into and left without walls.

Reflection Questions

1. Why do you think that a person without self-control is akin to a city without walls?

2. In the days when this verse was written, what types of dangers could come about as a result of not having any walls or barriers from outside influences?

3. What outside influences seem to affect your emotions? Television, music, coworkers?

ACTIVITY: IN CONTROL

Journal prompt: When I interact with someone who has no control over their emotions, it is...

This week, really focus on being self-controlled. What are some major things you must work on (e.g., your tongue, feeling bored with life, sadness, your rage, your time)? Choose something you really need to work on, and ensure you are being controlled in that area this week.

Refuse to allow your emotions to rule your life or keep you in bad moods or spaces.

Of course, we aren't always happy, and that's just a part of life, but we still must press forward. We can't allow these emotions to create stagnation in our lives.

What emotion are you taking charge of this week?

Pray for emotional stability and control of your tongue.

Proverbs 18:21 I James 1:26 I Proverbs 21:23 I Proverbs 29:11 I Proverbs 15:18

WEEK TWENTY-SEVEN

SHE IS A SEXUAL BEING

Sex is a large aspect of marriage that unfortunately many times is glossed over when speaking to singles. Of course, as single women our goal is to not fornicate, and to have repented of this sin if we have in the past. Both men and women are sexual beings, and this is something important to discuss with your husband-to-be, as it will certainly play a large role in your union.

Scripture Memorization

Genesis 2:24 — Therefore a man shall leave his father and his mother and hold fast to his wife and they shall become one flesh.

Reflection Questions

1. What are some questions you will ask your to-be-husband when you meet that pertain to sex?

2. How was sex introduced to you growing up? Did someone discuss it with you, or did you have to learn about it on your own? How do you think this hindered or benefited you as an adult?

3. Are you comfortable with speaking about sex with your significant other? If not, what makes you feel uncomfortable?

4. On a scale of 1–10, how important do you think sex is in marriage?

ACTIVITY: LET'S TALK ABOUT SEX

Journal prompt: *If I could go back and change something about my sexual history, it would be ...*

Make a list of three questions you want to ask your significant other about sex after you get married.

Also, if you haven't already this year, get tested! It's important to know your status with STIs and STDs so you aren't passing things along unknowingly. If you aren't able to go to a testing facility this week, at least make an appointment for the future.

1.

2.

3.

Pray for sexual purity before marriage and a healthy sex life after.

1 Corinthians 7:3–5 I Hebrews 13:4 I 1 Corinthians 7:2 I Proverbs 5:18–19

WEEK TWENTY-EIGHT

SHE IS RESPECTFUL

One of the things a godly wife is charged to do is to respect her husband. She respects him as a leader, husband, and man of God. Respect is defined as a feeling of deep admiration for someone or something elicited by their abilities, qualities or achievements. When we initially meet and begin dating, we usually have the utmost respect for our partners. As time goes on, that respect may wane. It is important to be consistent in your respect for your husband as you are commanded by God to do so.

Scripture Memorization

Ephesians 5:33 — However, let each of you love his wife as himself, and let the wife see that she respects her husband.

Reflection Questions

1. Why are women specifically told to respect their husbands? Why do you think respect is so important for a man? What does a marriage look like when the woman has no respect for her husband?

2. The Bible tells us that the man is the head of the household (1 Corinthians 11:3). How does this make you feel?

3. What is your definition of respect?

ACTIVITY: ALL ABOUT RESPECT

Journal prompt: When someone disrespects me, it makes me...

Many men say that respect to them is akin to showing love, just as we learned earlier that we show love to Jesus through obedience.

This week make it a point to pay attention to the way you respect others. Whom do you respect and why? What in them makes you feel as if they should be respected? On the flip side, pay attention to when you don't feel like respecting someone or are disrespectful. Why do you think this was the case? Make notes below.

> Pray for God to reveal what it means to respect a man.

Romans 12:9–11 | 1 Peter 2:17 | 1 Corinthians 11:3 | 1 Thessalonians 5:12–13

Monthly Check-in

Did I keep up with my God-plan this month?

Do I feel like I'm truly ready for a marriage? Why or why not?

What are some things the activities so far have brought to my attention that I still have to grow in as a woman of God who desires marriage?

Is there anything positive that has occurred as a result of my studies or closer connection with God this month?

TESTIMONY TO SHARE:

Notes

Eight

SHE IS WEAK

Month Eight

She opens her mouth with wisdom, and the teaching of kindness is on her tongue.

Proverbs 31:26

The Bible tells us in 2 Corinthians 12:9 that God's strength is made perfect in our weakness. God uses our weakness to show His strength, and a wise, godly wife knows this fact. It is not in her own strength that she is able to make it through tough times, but in her weakness, she leans on God for power. In the readings, we see varying accounts of the same story: a woman who understood she need only to reach God for strength.

READINGS

- Matthew 9:20–22
- Mark 5:25–34
- Luke 8:43–48

Group Questions

1. Compare and contrast the three versions of this story.

   _____
   _____
   _____

2. From touching Jesus's garment, the woman was healed from the issue of blood, but she had to have faith, and she had to do the work of pursuing Jesus to get to Him. How difficult do you think it was for her as a sickly woman to push through the crowd just to touch the hem of His garment?

   _____
   _____
   _____

3. Is there anything you can take away and use from this woman's perseverance?

   _____
   _____

4. Why do you think faith is such a large aspect of being a Christ follower? Why do you think it means so much to God that we have faith in Him?

_____
_____
_____
_____

5. When you have an issue, whom do you usually find yourself having faith to run to? Is it your parents, friends, yourself, or God? How can you ensure that God is your first go-to in the future?

_____
_____
_____
_____

6. Jesus's response to her was not what the woman expected, as she was fearful to approach Him. Why do you think she was afraid?

_____
_____
_____
_____

7. How can you learn from the woman when approaching God with things you may be ashamed of or fearful of telling Him? How do you think He will respond to you as His child?

_____
_____
_____
_____

GROUP ACTIVITY: Forgiven

What are some things you seek to be forgiven of or must forgive yourself for? Write down at least three things.

To take it further: Have an altar call and leave them on the altar today.

WEEK TWENTY-NINE

SHE IS FORGIVING

Forgiveness plays a large part in letting go of past issues, pains, and traumas. It is also prerequisite in our walk with God because as Christians we are called to be extremely forgiving people. A godly woman forgives not only because she is commanded by God but also because He forgives us. It is such an important part of the Christian walk that if we haven't forgiven someone, the Bible tells us we need to do so before we begin to pray (Mark 11:25). Forgiveness gives us the ability to move on and not remain stagnant in anger or bitterness. Imagine how much better your life would be if you didn't feel sad, hurt, angry, or bitter about that issue that someone caused you, no matter how long ago it occurred. Forgiveness is freedom.

Scripture Memorization

Matthew 6:14 — For if you forgive others their trespasses, your heavenly Father will also forgive you.

Reflection Questions

1. Can you think of any examples of unforgiveness in the Bible? How did this turn out for the people who refused to forgive?

2. Why is forgiveness more so for the person doing the forgiving, than the person who needs to be forgiven?

3. How important is forgiveness in marriage? Imagine you married an extremely unforgiving person; how pleasant do you think the relationship would be?

ACTIVITY: FORGIVE & FORGET

Journal prompt: If unforgiveness were an object, it would be...

Make a list of at least two to three people you need to forgive today. It may even be yourself for making some decisions you feel weren't the smartest. Then write a letter or paragraph to them expressing three things:

- *The pain they caused you*
- *Why you are forgiving them*
- *How you would like to proceed with the relationship, if at all*

Forgiveness is a practice that is usually progressive, so if you don't feel you have fully let it go right away, as is usually the case, don't be hard on yourself. Just know that you are on the right path by wanting to forgive.

> Pray that God would put anyone on your heart who you need to forgive.

Ephesians 4:32 I Mark 11:25 I 1 John 1:9 I Matthew 6:15

WEEK THIRTY

SHE IS BROKEN

In a previous chapter, we discussed the godly wife being a woman of strength, but she also possesses a weakness—this weakness is present because she knows she is only strong because of the God she worships. She allows Him to work through her and gains her strength from him. Her strength comes from the Lord. Our biblical example for this month exemplifies this in that she realized her healing came from God, not man and not through her own strength.

Scripture Memorization

Psalm 147:3 – He heals the brokenhearted and binds up their wounds.

Reflection Questions

1. When have you found yourself needing to rely on God's strength? Was it difficult or easy?

2. In the story of the woman with the issue of blood, we see a woman desperate for healing. Have you ever been or known someone who was seeking healing and received it? If so, share with your study group.

3. Read 2 Corinthians 12:9–10. What does Paul say about his weakness?

4. How do you think being a broken woman restored by God is beneficial in a marriage?

ACTIVITY: WE ALL FALL

Journal prompt:
Heartbreak can turn out to be a good thing when...

Just like we recognized our strengths, we must recognize the privilege and honor of our weaknesses. Imagine that you are interviewing the Proverbs 31 woman about how she gains her strength, overcomes trials and deals with marital issues. Come up with at least five questions.

1. _____

2. _____

3. _____

4. _____

5. _____

Now take these questions and interview two married women you know and trust. They may be mentors, coworkers, friends, or from your church. Ask them the questions you came up with for your interview. Share what you learn with your study group.

Pray, thanking God for your supernatural healing and strength.

Jeremiah 17:14 | Isaiah 41:10 | Jeremiah 33:6 | Psalm 103:2–4 | Psalm 73:26

WEEK THIRTY-ONE

SHE IS IMPERFECT

People in general recognize that their humanity makes them imperfect. A woman of God understands that with this humanity comes imperfection, but she has a Creator who still loves her. She will make mistakes, but she is also gentle with herself. We all sin and fall short, we miss the mark. God knows this will happen—and that is why we should be so grateful for grace and the fact that He loves us anyway.

Scripture Memorization

1 John 1:9 — If we confess our sins, he is faithful and just to forgive us our sins and to cleanse us from all unrighteousness.

Reflection Questions

1. Why do you think it is so important to confess your sins?

2. Do you allow space for others' humanness? Are you as understanding with others' imperfections as you would like them to be with you?

3. Husbands are extremely imperfect, as are wives! How can you make it a point to be understanding in your marriage? What things can you work on now when dealing with others that will carry over into marriage?

ACTIVITY: WHAT I WISH I KNEW

Journal prompt: When I focus on my good characteristics or my imperfections, I feel...

What are some things you wish you knew about life in general when you were younger? Write your younger self a short letter below about life and anything you would want her to be aware of. Tell her about your tests, trials, and lessons, and touch on how she should deal with imperfections.

Pray for acceptance of yourself the way you are.

Ephesians 2:8 I Romans 5:8 I James 3:2 I Ecclesiastes 7:20

WEEK THIRTY-TWO

SHE IS A FOLLOWER

A requirement of being a Christian woman is to follow Jesus. We are to walk as He walked, talk as He talked, and imitate Him while we have the opportunity here on earth (1 Peter 2:21; 1 Corinthians 11:1). We are to be representations of Him, and we do that through getting to know Him through Scripture reading and prayer.

Scripture Memorization

John 8:12 — Again Jesus spoke to them, saying, "I am the light of the world. Whoever follows me will not walk in darkness, but will have the light of life."

Reflection Questions

1. Imagine you are living when Jesus walked the earth. Where do you think you would have fit into the picture? Would you have been a follower or someone who watched from the sidelines?

2. Why do you think it is important that we have little regard for this life as a follower of Jesus?

3. Why is it important to be equally yoked in a marriage?

ACTIVITY: FOLLOW THE LEADER

Journal prompt: *If Jesus showed up at my door and told me to leave my life and follow Him, I would...*

Using the chart below, summarize the Bible verses about being a follower of Jesus. Decide if you truly in your heart are prepared to do these things to follow Him.

VERSE	SUMMARY	YES OR NO
Mark 8:34		
1 John 2:3–4		
Matthew 4:19		
John 12:26		
Matthew 10:34–39		
John 15:18–21		
John 14:23		
John 13:34–35		
Matthew 19:21		

Pray for the courage to follow Jesus wherever He asks you to go

John 12:26 | Mark 8:34 | 1 John 2:27 | Matthew 4:19

Monthly Check-in

How much time did I spend with God this month?

Do I feel healing still needs to be done from a previous grievance? How can I go about beginning the healing process? Come up with a long-term plan.

What is my strategy for shifting heart motives still needed to become a true follower of God?

Is there anything positive that has occurred as a result of my studies or closer connection with God this month?

TESTIMONY TO SHARE:

Notes

Nine

SHE UNDERSTANDS THERE IS MORE

Month Nine

She extends her hand to the poor, and she stretches out her hands to the needy.

Proverbs 31:20

As Christians we understand that it is not all about us--our desires, and our wants--but about what God has sent us to do with this time. There are times when we don't want to do the things we are called to do as women, wives, and Christians. We may have to search a little deeper for the internal fortitude that lives inside of us through the Holy Spirit to be brave enough to face some challenges. In the next passage, we read about a woman who had to do just that.

READING

- Esther 3–8

Group Questions

1. Imagine you are Esther. How would you respond in this situation? Why do you think she responded the way she did—out of fear or love for her people?

   _____
   _____
   _____
   _____

2. Fasting is such a gift and a huge aspect of our Christian walk. Why do you think it is used many times throughout the Bible in times of turmoil or fear or before battles? How do you integrate fasting into your life?

   _____
   _____
   _____
   _____

3. Haman wound up being put to death on the very gallows prepared for Mordecai. What can you take away from this about the way God works on our behalf?

_____

_____

_____

_____

_____

_____

4. Sometimes God calls us to do great things that we may not feel adequately prepared to do or may not even have the desire to do. What do you think Esther had to overcome internally before putting her life on the line for her people? What can you take away from this internal fortitude to use in your own life (e.g., you work a job you hate but God has you there to help others; or you have a family member you don't like to interact with who shows up to all the family functions, but you will be the only Jesus they see.) How can you put your own feelings and desires aside to ensure you are doing what God has called you to do for such a time as this?

_____

_____

_____

_____

5. Even being the queen, Esther could not go and see the king unless summoned. Death was usually a consequence of this act. But the king allowed her to speak, as he obviously cared for her and respected her opinion. What qualities in Esther do you think the king saw in her to respect what she had to say? Do you think those qualities still apply to today's marriages?

_____

_____

_____

_____

_____

_____

ACTIVITY: Date Night

What are some ways you can show your husband that you love him? Dream up anything you would like (e.g., treating him to his favorite restaurant, having a candlelight picnic in the backyard, giving him time to watch the game). Think of ways you two can spend time together or how you can make him feel special.

One full day of

WEEK THIRTY-THREE

SHE SACRIFICES TIME

Of all the things a wife, mother, and woman of God sacrifices, her time is one of the most precious and valuable. This is because it is something she cannot get back. As a woman who is always about doing God's work, she is most likely putting something else aside to sacrifice her time for others.

Scripture Memorization

Hebrews 13:16 — Do not neglect to do good and to share what you have, for such sacrifices are pleasing to God.

Reflection Questions

1. Why do you think it is important to sacrifice time as a Christian woman?

2. When you don't want to do something, do you find yourself giving the task your all, or is it usually a halfhearted attempt?

3. Why is the sacrifice of time so important in marriage?

ACTIVITY: DEAL BREAKERS

Journal prompt: *My time is precious because…*

Giving of yourself completely to someone, as in marriage, takes a lot of courage and is a bold leap of faith. It is not a step to be taken lightly. Although divorce has now become a common option, it is still hated by God! That is why it is so important to take your time when becoming engaged and eventually married. The main reason, in most cases, for dating or courting is to get to know someone prior to marriage. You want to have a vision for your dating and married life, but to do that you need to start with your deal breakers.

List some of them on the next page, then take those deal breakers and make them into a dating questionnaire.

Pray to use your time wisely.

Hebrews 13:16 I Philippians 2:4 I 2 Corinthians 9:7 I John 15:13

MY DEAL BREAKERS

1.
2.
3.
4.
5.
6.
7.
8.
9.
10.

1.

2.

3.

4.

5.

6.

7.

8.

9.

10.

WEEK THIRTY-FOUR

SHE FINDS HER *WHY*

The godly wife understands that her *why* is bigger than her life and goals. She understands that all she does in life is for a greater cause beyond her desires. This includes her desire to enter into marriage. She knows that marriage is not just for her benefit and to fulfill her desire of having a spouse. Ultimately, all that she does is for the benefit of God and His kingdom.

Memorization Verse

John 8:12 — Again Jesus spoke to them, saying, "I am the light of the world. Whoever follows me will not walk in darkness, but will have the light of life."

Reflection Questions

1. Why do you think it is so important to find your *why* beyond the selfish reasons of wanting things because you want them?

2. What does the world say our *why* should be for wanting money, marriage, or most things in life?

3. Why is it important to determine prior to entering a union *why* you want to be married?

ACTIVITY: FINDING WHY

Journal prompt: *My dreams are not just for me, but for…*

Beyond having an extravagant wedding and donning a gorgeous wedding ring, what is your why for wanting children, the beautiful wedding, or the marriage you desire? What is your *why* for pursuing the goals and dreams you currently are pursuing? Is it for more than money? Is it to put you in position to do God's work? Come up with a sentence or two describing your *why*.

Put it aside and come back to it the next day or a couple of days later, and decide if changes are necessary.

Pray for clear understanding of your why & to align it to God's vision.

1 Timothy 5:8 I Psalm 127:3–5 I Ecclesiastes 4:9 I Proverbs 27:17

WEEK THIRTY-FIVE

SHE USES HER POSITION TO BENEFIT THE KINGDOM

We are born at a specific time and place that God ordained. The Bible tells us that He knew us before we were in the womb and He knitted us together for His purpose. We are to use our resources and positions to benefit His kingdom, just as Esther chose to do.

Scripture Memorization

1 Peter 4:10 — As each has received a gift, use it to serve one another, as good stewards of God's varied grace.

Reflection Questions

1. In the story of Esther, we see that she was placed in the palace for a specific reason. It reminds us that we are where we are for a reason. You were born at this time and place for a reason, and God placed you in your specific position for such a time as this. What do you think your God-given reason could be, in your current position, to benefit His kingdom?

2. We see that Esther had a choice to make in whether she would use her position as the queen to help her people. How difficult would it have been for you to make this decision?

3. How can your position as a godly wife be used to benefit the kingdom of God?

ACTIVITY: SWITCHING POSITIONS

Journal prompt: *When I'm in a situation or job with people I'm not that fond of, I immediately want to…*

What gifts do you have? Write a list. What are your God-given talents? Speaking, writing, organizing? List two or more things you are naturally good at.

If you are having trouble with this, you can take a spiritual gifts quiz online or ask someone close to you whom you trust to help you determine something you are good at.

Determine how you can use these gifts for the kingdom of God in your current position.

Pray for wisdom to use your current career to benefit the kingdom.

1 Corinthians 6:20 I Matthew 5:16 I Ephesians 2:10 I Galatians 6:14

WEEK THIRTY-SIX

SHE UNDERSTANDS THE POWER IN HER FEMINIITY

As women we have the power of femininity! It is important to understand the power that comes along with being a woman and use it for good. Femininity can be used as a manipulative weapon or to exhibit the power of love. It is up to you how you will embrace your femininity.

Scripture Memorization

1 Peter 3:7 — Likewise, husbands, live with your wives in an understanding way, showing honor to the woman as the weaker vessel, since they are heirs with you of the grace of life, so that your prayers may not be hindered.

Reflection Questions

1. Have you used your femininity in manipulative ways in the past? What was the result? Did anyone get hurt—you or the other person or both?

2. What are some of the strengths and weaknesses of femininity and masculinity?

3. How can understanding your feminine power before entering a marriage be beneficial to your husband?

4. How can you ensure you use your feminine power in marriage as tool of love and not as a weapon?

ACTIVITY: THE POWER OF A WOMAN

Journal prompt: I am happy that God made me a woman because…

Read the Bible passages below and determine how the women used their feminine power. The last space was left blank for you to find another biblical example.

BIBLE PASSAGE

GENESIS 29:16–30

2 SAMUEL 11

HOSEA 1–3

JUDGES 13–16

Pray for a pure heart and to use your gift of femininity wisely

Judges 13–16 | Genesis 29:16–30 | 2 Samuel 11 | Hosea 1–3

Monthly Check-in

Did I keep up with my God-plan this month?

What are three things I learned about myself this month?

How can I ensure that I am pursuing things not just for selfish reasons but for the benefit of God and His kingdom, as I am called to put Him first in all I do?

Is there anything positive that has occurred as a result of my studies or closer connection with God this month?

TESTIMONY TO SHARE:

Notes

Ten

SHE FINDS HER TRIBE

Month Ten

*Her children rise up and call her blessed;
her husband also, and he praises her*

Proverbs 31:28

Women often find like-minded women to talk to and bond with. As women of God, we have the added benefit of bonding over the things of God and producing positive, beneficial friendships that last a lifetime. It is often said that "your tribe attracts your vibe"—and it is so true. Good friends can help lift us up when we're down, speak a needed word into our lives, or simply be a shoulder to cry on. That is why it is important to surround yourself with people who are uplifting, encouraging, and wise, like the women in the following readings.

READINGS

- Luke 8:1–3
- Acts 16:14–15

Group Questions

1. Do you feel having friendship is an important aspect of your life? Why or why not?

   _____
   _____
   _____
   _____

2. What is a *tribe* to you? What denotes close friendship to you?

   _____
   _____
   _____
   _____

3. The common denominator that drew these women toward their tribes was Jesus and the word of God. When you think about your closest friendships, what is the main common denominator?

_____

_____

_____

_____

4. These friendships had purpose. What would you say the purpose was?

_____

_____

_____

_____

5. What do you feel the purpose of friendship should be? Is this purpose true for many of your friendships?

_____

_____

_____

6. Jesus was rarely alone. The Bible tells us He was always teaching and interacting with others. Since we are to model our lives after His, how does this tell us we are to interact with others?

_____

_____

_____

_____

NOTES

ACTIVITY: Circle of Love

If you didn't already know the women in your group, hopefully you have gotten to know them well. Now is going to be a time to love on them as tribe members should.

Sitting in a circle, one person sits in the center, and everyone writes down positive things about this person (one or two positive characteristics) on sticky notes. The person receives them and reads each one out loud.

Make sure to use sticky notes because you are going to attach them to the next page!

To take it further: Try this at home with your family or at work with your coworkers!

STICKY NOTES

WEEK THIRTY-SEVEN

SHE SEEKS WISE MENTORSHIP

Regardless of what you pursue in life, research shows that having wise counsel and mentorship increases your chances of success. This is no difference in marriage and your Christian walk. While God is always our Head, it is smart to seek wise counsel. The Bible tells us multiple times that it is smart to seek wise counsel and those who don't are considered fools (Proverbs 12:15). It also states that our plans fail without counsel (Proverbs 15:22). With marriage and family-building being two of the most important life decisions we make, why hinder your journey by not seeking the advice of someone who has been there and done that?

Scripture Memorization

Titus 2:3 — Older women likewise are to be reverent in behavior not slanderers or slaves to much wine. They are to teach what is good.

Reflection Questions

1. Whom can you identify as key mentors you've had in your life?

2. Looking at the verses for this week, why do you think having wise counsel is so important?

3. How many times have you looked back and wished you had done something differently? Do you think having wise counsel would have been helpful?

ACTIVITY: SHOW ME THE WAY

Journal prompt: *I have a hard time letting people in at times because ...*

Complete the Pros and Cons list regarding mentorship. If it helps, look at some of the research about mentorship and how it helps or hinders people. If you haven't already, decide to seek out wise mentorship this week in the area of relationships or spirituality.

PROS	CONS

Pray for wise mentors

Proverbs 20:18 I Proverbs 13:10 I Galatians 6:2 I 1 Timothy 2:2–5

WEEK THIRTY-EIGHT

SHE FELLOWSHIPS

Fellowshipping with other believers can come about in many ways: Bible studies at one another's homes, outings with others, and commonly, through church or church events. Regular fellowship is obviously something we are not to take lightly or for granted since it is mentioned in the Bible. As humans we desire companionship and should enjoy being around others just as much as we enjoy our quiet time alone.

Scripture Memorization

Hebrews 10:24–25 — And let us consider how to stir up one another to love and good works, not neglecting to meet together, as is the habit of some, but encouraging one another, and all the more as you see the Day drawing near.

Reflection Questions

1. What do you think church and fellowship looked like at the time when Jesus walked the earth? Do you think it was similar to today?

2. Do you find it important to fellowship with other believers? Why or why not?

3. What does Paul say the purpose of fellowship is? Do you feel your church agrees and acts on this stance?

ACTIVITY: OUT WITH THE OLD

Journal prompt: I first realized the people at church were only human when…

When you are married, your husband becomes your head, and technically, he is your closest family as the two become one. This may take some adjusting to after you have walked down the aisle and said your vows. I've often heard it said that a woman gives up so much when she marries. But if it is a God-ordained marriage, it's worth it. Yet it is good to be realistic about matters like marriage. Just as Sarah left her family to go with Abraham, many wives leave their own churches to attend their husband's, under a united house. What other things do you think you will have to sacrifice or let go of once you are married?

Make a list of some of the major changes that will come with marriage, and show it to someone you trust who has been married for a while. Is there anything they would add to that list that you may not have thought of? Keep in mind that every marriage is different, and part of the joy of the journey is getting to know your husband and what you expect from each other as husband and wife, as you both give up some of the old to embrace something new.

Pray for those in your church family.

1 John 1:3 I Matthew 18:20 I 1 John 1:7 I Acts 2:42 I Proverbs 27:17

WEEK THIRTY-NINE

SHE IS A MENTOR

We discussed finding mentorship in a previous chapter, but it is also important to be spending time giving back as a mentor. Therefore, it is vital that as women of God we are seeking His wisdom from above. We seek wisdom not only to make wise decisions for ourselves but to pass along that wisdom to others to help them in their journeys.

Scripture Memorization

Titus 2:4–5 — And so train the young women to love their husbands and children, to be self-controlled, pure, working at home, kind, and submissive to their own husbands, that the word of God may not be reviled.

Reflection Questions

1. While it is easy to understand the importance of mentorship, why do you think it is equally important that you are able to mentor others in their walk?

2. What are some of the pros and cons of being a mentor?

3. Identify a mentor in the Bible. It could be Eli, Paul, or anyone else you choose. How did they speak into the lives of the people they mentored? How did they help them grow?

4. When you think of a great husband, is mentorship something that comes to mind? Why or why not?

ACTIVITY: PASS IT ON

Journal prompt: *I feel I will be a good mentor because...*

Take some time to complete the survey below.
Pray about and seek out opportunities to mentor others.

1. Something I have been through that I can share with others is...

2. I would feel comfortable mentoring others in this setting...

3. I enjoy working with this age range...

4. Does my church have or need a mentor program currently?

5. My biggest barrier to being a mentor is...

Pray to be a positive mentor to others and for godly guidance.

2 Timothy 3:16–17 I 2 Timothy 4:2 I 1 Timothy 4:13 I Titus 2:3–5

WEEK FORTY

SHE IS HAPPY FOR OTHERS' SUCCESSES

If we interact with others in any situation, it is inevitable that we'll encounter attitudes, insecurities, and envy. Sometimes, we may find ourselves acting out of our insecurities or jealousies. In the story of Peninnah and Hannah (1 Samuel 1:1–16), we see a clear case of jealousy. It was a tumultuous love triangle that left one woman in a depression! Stories like this teach us that we must protect our hearts and the hearts of those around us. In James 3:14 we see that if we harbor any bitter jealousy or selfish ambition, this is not from God. A woman of God is mature in relationship and deals with conflict, issues of jealousy, or envy on her own part or with others.

Scripture Memorization

1 Corinthians 13:11 — When I was a child, I spoke like a child, I thought like a child, I reasoned like a child. When I became a man, I gave up childish ways.

Reflection Questions

1. Have you recently encountered an issue where your maturity was tested? Did you react with godly wisdom?

2. How did Hannah deal with the issues between her and Peninnah?

3. How do you usually find yourself dealing with jealousy and envy on your part? Is it helping or hindering your walk?

4. Where do jealously and envy come from?

ACTIVITY: MAKING AMENDS

Journal prompt: Not always being mentally and spiritually mature has cost me...

Not many people are completely immune to the comparison game. There may be times when we find that our hearts are envious or jealous of someone else. If we do harbor feelings of resentment or anger toward someone, we often come off as being mean, harsh, or fake in our interactions with them (even if we don't mean to). This is not in accordance with the heart of a Christian woman. Even if that person is intentionally trying to rile those feelings in you, you have to get them under control.

If you find yourself feeling envious or jealous of someone else because of what they have or the way they look, pray for them. If it is someone on social media you don't know well, unfollow them.

If you have done anything to hurt or offend anyone you were envious or jealous of, you must take responsibility for your actions and truly seek forgiveness through apology. Everyone has something special and unique about them—you are no different. Always remember that!

This week take some time to reflect on someone you may have been treating unfairly or wrongly. This could be someone extremely close to you or someone you see every once in a while. Make amends with them if possible.

Pray for maturity in any area needed & for those who you may envy.

1 Corinthians 14:20 I 1 Corinthians 13:11 I Ephesians 4:14–15 I Hebrews 6:1–3

Monthly Check-in

Did I keep up with my God-plan this month?

How am I fellowshipping adequately?

What is my strategy for becoming a mature woman of God?

Is there anything positive that has occurred as a result of my studies or closer connection with God this month?

TESTIMONY TO SHARE:

Notes

Eleven

SHE IS A WOMAN OF EXCELLENCE

Month Eleven

Many women do noble things,
but you surpass them all.

Proverbs 31:29

Proverbs 31 is an extremely well-known Bible passage, but this does not mean it should be glossed over. Take some time to really delve into what the Proverbs 31 woman represents. Although it may be nearly impossible to embody all these attributes at one time, we can surely try as godly wives.

Reading

- Proverbs 31

Group Questions

1. Who is speaking in Proverbs 31, and to whom?

   _____
   _____
   _____

2. Do you think that being a Proverbs 31 woman is achievable? In your opinion, is it an attainment worth achieving?

   _____
   _____
   _____
   _____
   _____

3. How would you describe her in your own words? What are some major qualities she embodies?

   _____
   _____

4. Do you know any women who resemble the Proverbs 31 woman? If you don't know of one personally, can you think of someone famous you perceive in this way? What about them gives you this perception?

5. Saying the Proverbs 31 woman is a hard worker would be an understatement; many of the verses focus on her work ethic. In what areas of your life are you like her, and in what areas of your life do you need to be more diligent?

6. King Lemuel's mother and the Proverbs 31 woman that she describes seem to be very wise women. What do you envision their prayer life and walk with God to look like?

7. What is said about her husband in the passage? How does she treat him? What does he think of her?

GROUP ACTIVITY: 31 Ways

Take the verses from Proverbs 31:10–31 and ascribe an adjective to each verse that describes her. Make a list of all 22 adjectives. Check off one or more that you want to focus on developing this month.

		VERSE (NIV)	ADJECTIVE
	10	A wife of noble character who can find? She is worth far more than rubies.	
	11	Her husband has full confidence in her and lacks nothing of value.	
	12	She brings him good, not harm, all the days of her life.	
	13	She selects wool and flax and works with eager hands.	
	14	She is like the merchant ships, bringing her food from afar.	
	15	She gets up while it is still night; she provides food for her family and portions for her female servants.	
	16	She considers a field and buys it; out of her earnings she plants a vineyard.	
	17	She sets about her work vigorously; her arms are strong for her tasks.	
	18	She sees that her trading is profitable, and her lamp does not go out at night.	
	19	In her hand she holds the distaff and grasps the spindle with her fingers.	
	20	She opens her arms to the poor and extends her hands to the needy.	
	21	When it snows, she has no fear for her household; for all of them are clothed in scarlet.	
	22	She makes coverings for her bed; she is clothed in fine linen and purple.	
	23	Her husband is respected at the city gate, where he takes his seat among the elders of the land.	
	24	She makes linen garments and sells them, and supplies the merchants with sashes.	

	25	She is clothed with strength and dignity; she can laugh at the days to come.	
	26	She speaks with wisdom, and faithful instruction is on her tongue.	
	27	She watches over the affairs of her household and does not eat the bread of idleness.	
	28	Her children arise and call her blessed; her husband also, and he praises her.	
	29	"Many women do noble things, but you surpass them all."	
	30	Charm is deceptive, and beauty is fleeting; but a woman who fears the Lord is to be praised.	
	31	Honor her for all that her hands have done, and let her works bring her praise at the city gate.	

Take it further: Make a list of 12 character traits you desire to possess, and work on one a month for the year!

WEEK FORTY-ONE

SHE IS HOLY IN CONDUCT

Being holy is a matter of the heart. There is no one-size-fits-all godly woman, but there are some guidelines the Bible points out that a godly wife, or any woman of God, should possess, and holiness is one of them. Just look at Martha and Mary. They were sisters but were very different in the way they handled and expressed themselves. God made each of us with our own unique characteristics, quirks, and features. In no way are we meant to be cookie cutter.

Scripture Memorization

Leviticus 20:26 — You are to be holy to me for I the Lord am holy and have separated you from the peoples, that you should be mine.

Reflection Questions

1. How difficult do you find it to be "set apart" as holy in your single walk? What is the bright side?

2. What does it mean to be holy?

3. How can this time of being set apart prepare you for the marriage you desire?

ACTIVITY: SET APART

Journal prompt: When I think of the word "holy," the first thing that comes to mind is …

The Bible states that we are called to be holy, and God sets the holy apart. If you are single, this means we shouldn't be so quick to jump into a relationship. If it is not ordained by God, is it a relationship you would really want anyway? Find out what else the Bible says about being holy, and discern what this means for your life. Use the chart below to keep track of what you find. Keep the Scriptures with you this week and meditate on them.

SCRIPTURE	WHAT IT MEANS FOR ME

Pray for holiness in your walk

1 Peter 1:14–16 **I** 1 Peter 3:5 **I** 1 Corinthians 3:16–17 **I** Hebrews 12:14

WEEK FORTY-TWO

SHE POSSESSES THE FRUIT OF THE SPIRIT

A woman who possesses the fruit of the Spirit is one with wisdom, vibrancy, and happiness. She knows that whatever comes at her, she has the tools to respond like a gentle woman of the Lord. A woman who regularly practices the fruit of the Spirit leads a life that is pleasing in God's sight.

Scripture Memorization

Galatians 5:22–23 — But the fruit of the Spirit is love, joy, peace, forbearance, kindness, goodness, faithfulness, gentleness and self-control. Against such things there is no law.

Reflection Questions

1. Why do you think it is important in this day to have the fruit of the Spirit? In your everyday life? In your marriage?

2. Which fruits of the Spirit do you feel you possess?

3. How do you acquire the fruit of the Spirit?

ACTIVITY: FRUITS & FLESH

Journal prompt: I do not act like a person who has the Fruit of the Spirit when I...

Look at the list of the fruit of the Spirit below and next to that the works of the flesh.

Circle, highlight, or check off the fruits of the Spirit that you need growth in and any fruits of the flesh you need to let go of and surrender to God. Really focus on starting the journey to do just that this week. As a bonus challenge, memorize the Fruit of the Spirit if you haven't already; quiz others in your study group the next time you meet!

FRUIT OF THE SPIRIT	FRUIT OF THE FLESH
Love	Adultery/Immorality
Joy	Fornication
Peace	Uncleanness/Impurity
Patience	Sensuality
Kindness	Idolatry
Goodness	Witchcraft/Sorcery
Faithfulness	Hatred/Enmities
Gentleness	Variance/Strife
Self-control	Jealousy
	Outbursts of anger
	Disputes
	Dissensions
	Factions
	Envy
	Drunkenness
	Carousing

Pray to grow in the Fruit of the Spirit

Matthew 3:8 | Galatians 5:16 | Galatians 5:19–21 | 2 Timothy 1:7

WEEK FORTY-THREE

SHE LOVES WITHOUT FEAR

God is love, and we see the biggest sacrifice in the Bible when Jesus loved us enough to give His life so we may have the opportunity to spend eternity with Him. As Christians, we are called to love one another, and a godly wife understands that being loving is one of her greatest callings. She loves God, her family, her community, and herself!

Remember, it is key to express love for your husband in a way he would recognize. If he is not into receiving gifts and would rather have your time, then no matter how many ties you buy him, he won't see that as being loved but as a nice gesture. Love is not selfish.

Scripture Memorization

1 John 4:18 — There is no fear in love, but perfect love casts out fear. For fear has to do with punishment, and whoever fears has not been perfected in love.

Reflection Questions

1. Read 1 Corinthians 13:4–7. Do you think the type of love described in those verses is truly feasible in a marriage today?

2. Why can there be no fear in perfect love?

3. Why did Jesus not entrust Himself completely to mankind, even though He loves them. What does this say about the way we are to love?

4. Have you seen good examples of the type of love described in the Bible? If so, share at your next group study.

ACTIVITY: LOVE IS

Journal prompt: *I am afraid to love without fear because…*

Take the Scripture challenge! Read through 1 Corinthians 13:4–7, and anywhere you see the words "love" or "it," replace with your name. Think back to your most recent previous relationships and compare your actions and thoughts with what the Bible says love is. Try this week to be more loving toward others. Always keep in mind how the Bible describes love.

1 Corinthians 13:4–7

_____ is patient, _____ is kind. _____ does not envy, _____ does not boast, _____ is not proud. _____ does not dishonor others, _____ is not self-seeking, _____ is not easily angered, _____ keeps no record of wrongs. _____ does not delight in evil but rejoices with the truth. _____ always protects, always trusts, always hopes, always perseveres.

Pray for discernment and guidance in love

1 Corinthians 16:14; 13:2 I 1 John 4:8 I Colossians 3:14 I Romans 13:10

WEEK FORTY-FOUR

SHE WORSHIPS IN SPIRIT & TRUTH

In John 4:24, we are told that God is spirit, and those who worship Him must worship in spirit and truth. We are instructed as to how to worship in Romans 12:1–2. This is where we find out what true worship is. Take some time to read about worship God's way in the Bible.

Scripture Memorization

John 4:24 – God is spirit, and those who worship him must worship in spirit and truth.

Reflection Questions

1. What does it mean to you to "worship in spirit and truth"?

2. Why do you think worship means so much to God?

3. Is there anything else in your life you are worshiping, or idolizing, above God? How can you set it aside and truly repent?

ACTIVITY: WORSHIP WEEK

Journal prompt: *After worshiping God I feel...*

Every day this week, spend some time in worship. Read about worship in the Bible, and write down what you find below. Also, take some time to journal about your week of worship.

WHAT DOES GOD SAY ABOUT WORSHIP?

MY WEEK OF WORSHIP

Pray for guidance in worship.

Hebrews 13:15 | Romans 12:1 | John 4:23 | 1 Chronicles 16:29

WEEK FORTY-FIVE

SHE IS A BOSS

We see that the Proverbs 31 woman is a diligent, hard-working woman who got up before the sun and went to sleep late at night. She also made her own clothes, sold goods, and purchased her own land. Basically, she was a superwoman! She was an entrepreneur at heart and, obviously, a shrewd one.

Many women desire to accomplish similar things such as owning a business or having a successful corporate career, while others would rather work as stay-at-home moms. However you desire to live your life, finding the line between diligence and self-care is also an important aspect of being a godly wife.

Scripture Memorization

Colossians 3:23 — Whatever you do, work heartily, as for the Lord and not for men.

Reflection Questions

1. How can you use this Bible verse in the job you have now?

2. What does it mean to you to work heartily as for the Lord?

3. What is your ideal career path?

ACTIVITY: BOSS UP

Journal prompt: A boss is a woman who …

If you could do anything, what would it be? Dream big— there are no hindrances on what you could do!

What is one big thing you can do to put this dream into motion? Work on that this week!

Pray for knowledge, wisdom, and discernment in business and career.

Proverbs 16:3 I Proverbs 14:23 I Proverbs 18:9 I John 6:27

Monthly Check-in

Did I keep up with my God-plan this month?

How do I improve for next month?

What is my strategy for becoming a woman after God's own heart?

Is there anything positive that has occurred as a result of my studies or closer connection with God this month?

TESTIMONY TO SHARE:

Notes

Twelve

SHE IS BUSY ABOUT HER FATHER'S WORK

Month Twelve

Give her the product of her hands and let her works praise

Proverbs 31:31

Each of us, as women and children of God, has a purpose to fulfill with our time spent on earth. The women discussed in the following passages are only mentioned briefly, but what is said about them is significant. Each of them plays an important role in the world, no matter how big or small.

READINGS

- Romans 16:1–2
- Romans 16:3–5
- Romans 16:7

Group Questions

1. When you look at these three women—Junia, Priscilla, and Phoebe— what qualities or characteristics do you think they all possessed?

   _____
   _____
   _____
   _____

2. Paul states that Priscilla and Aquila were risking their own lives for his life, and Andronicus and Junia were imprisoned. How difficult do you think life was at that time, especially for Christians?

   _____
   _____
   _____
   _____

3. When you reflect on your own walk, what are some difficult things you've endured to help others come to Christ or to get the Word of God to someone?

4. We see that Junia was in Christ before Paul, so she probably remembered when Paul persecuted the Christians as Saul. How difficult do you think it was for her to forgive him and accept Paul? What does this relationship tell you about the Christian walk?

5. What can you take away from these three passages that can be used in your life?

6. How does Paul describe each of these people?

NOTES

Activity: Give Yourself Away

This activity is all about fully committing your life, will, and desires to God. Refer to the first activity on page 14, and rip the pages from the book—**yes, rip them out.** You are going to give them to God in prayer and take your hands off it. Decide how you and your Bible study mates will "let go" of your dreams and desires for your lives. Will you have a release party or burn them or simply rip them and throw them away? This is your life, but as a member of the body of Christ, it is now His life. With God as your Head, He has the ultimate say, which means things may not turn out or line up the way we see fit. If we really put God first in our lives, that means putting His desires above our own.

Make sure you pray before letting go. Ask for His will above all and for the strength and grace to truly submit to His will for your life. He loves us and does not want to see us in pain (how much more will He give to you) or sad (the Lord is near to the brokenhearted). But whatever happens concerning marriage, you must know and believe that it is in your best interest, as all things work together for good.

Take some time to answer the questions below and on the next page as a group.

> TO TAKE IT FURTHER: HAVE A RELEASE PARTY AFTER
> ANSWERING THE QUESTIONS BELOW!

1. What does it mean to truly give your life away?

2. Read Luke 22:42. How do you think Jesus felt in that moment, on the cross, knowing the burdens He had to bear? Why do you think He proceeded?

3. How do you feel about putting your dreams and desires in the hand of God? Be honest. Are you afraid, mad, sad, happy? Why do you feel this way?

4. How will you feel if marriage is not what God desires for your life?

WEEK FORTY-SIX

SHE SPREADS THE GOSPEL

People can observe many of the godly women in the Bible and know that they follow God because they talk about Him to others or they exude godly characteristics and traits. Take some time to look at other examples of godly women we did not touch on in the group studies this week.

Scripture Memorization

Mark 16:15 — And he said to them, "Go into all the world and proclaim the gospel to the whole creation."

Reflection Questions

1. If people examined your life and listened to you speak, would they automatically assume you were a follower of God?

2. If you were having a discussion with Jesus, who can see your heart and thoughts, would He say you were His follower?

3. How can you do your part to proclaim the gospel?

4. Are you hesitant about sharing the gospel with others? Why or why not?

5. How can you ensure your marriage is one where you both share the gospel with others?

ACTIVITY: ON A MISSION

Journal prompt: *If God told me to become a missionary, I would feel…*

Use the internet to research at least three stories of people on missions all over the globe. Alternatively, if you know someone or have a connection to someone who may have done missions work, interview them in person or via phone.

Get a feel for what it's like to be on a mission for God to spread His Word. Get a sense of the dangers of doing this in some areas of the world, and jot down your feelings.

Pray for God to guide you to the people He wants to know Him

Matthew 28:19 | Romans 1:16 | John 4:34 | 2 Timothy 4:2

WEEK FORTY-SEVEN

SHE SEEKS THE GIFTS OF GOD

A godly wife will always seek wisdom from God, even prior to getting married. As a godly wife, she will seek discernment and wisdom about who she should date, court, and eventually marry. To carry out God's will in our lives and marriages, we must have wisdom. When we speak with others and spread God's Word, we need His wisdom and discernment to guide our tongues.

Scripture Memorization

Proverbs 3:13–18 — Blessed is the one who finds wisdom, and the one who gets understanding, for the gain from her is better than gain from silver and her profit better than gold. She is more precious than jewels, and nothing you desire can compare with her. Long life is in her right hand; in her left hand are riches and honor. Her ways are ways of pleasantness, and all her paths are peace. She is a tree of life to those who lay hold of her; those who hold her fast are called blessed.

Reflection Questions

Scripture Questions:

1. What are the two types of wisdom found in the Bible?

2. How do we get godly wisdom?

3. Proverbs 3:13–18 states that wisdom is more precious than jewels. We heard something similar about a good wife being more precious than rubies (Proverbs 31:10)! Why do you think these two things—obtaining wisdom and being a good wife—are so invaluable?

ACTIVITY: MESSANGERS

Journal prompt: *A woman of wisdom is…*

This week, think of a way you can spread the gospel to those who may not have heard. Ask God to guide you and to give you discernment and wisdom. It may not be as drastic as going to a developing country, but it could be speaking to a friend who is in a rocky place, or if you are bold enough, grabbing some friends and taking it to the streets. You could start a blog or use a video platform to speak to people all over the world.

If you are nervous about speaking to people, one easy way to evangelize is to get tracts and pass them out to people or use them as a conversation starter. We are here to do God's work, and the main goal is to spread His Word no matter how far you travel.

Pray for godly wisdom, knowledge, and understanding.

James 3:17 I James 1:5 I 1 Thessalonians 5:21 I Proverbs 3:13–18

WEEK FORTY-EIGHT

SHE IS WALKING IN HER GOD-GIVEN PURPOSE

We were each given gifts to use here on earth, as we are told in 1 Peter 4:10, and we are to use those gifts to serve one another. Our gifts are not for us to selfishly hoard away but to be shared with the world. You do yourself and God a disservice when you don't share your gifts with the world. We are told in Colossians 3:17 that whatever we do, in word or deed, we should do everything in the name of the Lord Jesus. In 1 Corinthians 12 we see that there are a variety of gifts but the same Spirit, and there are varieties of service but the same Lord. Therefore, we are all using our gifts for the kingdom and working for the same boss—God.

Scripture Memorization

Romans 8:28 — And we know that for those who love God all things work together for good, for those who are called according to his purpose.

Reflection Questions

1. Read Jeremiah 29:11. Why do you think it was important for God to point out to Jeremiah that His plans were good? How would you live life if you truly believed this verse?

2. What does this verse tell us about those times we consider failures that may not work out as we intended?

3. How would you feel if you got to the end of your life and never truly walked in your purpose?

4. What things are currently keeping you from walking in your purpose?

ACTIVITY: PURPOSE & PRAYER

Journal prompt: When I am not walking in my purpose, I feel…

If you know your purpose, write it down. If you aren't walking in it, devise a plan to do so. Bring the plan with you to discuss at your next Bible study.

If you are still confused about your purpose, pray about it, and research reputable online "purpose" quizzes to help determine what your God-given purpose may be. If you have peace about a purpose that you know is from God, write down a brief plan to get started walking in your purpose.

MY PURPOSE PLAN

Pray for God to reveal or direct you in your purpose

Jeremiah 29:11 I Ecclesiastes 12:13–14 I Proverbs 16:4 I 1 Peter 2:9 I Psalm 138:8

WEEK FORTY-NINE

SHE GIVES HER LIFE AWAY

A woman of God realizes her life is not her own. She understands she belongs to God, and that includes her body, her desires, her goals, her missions, and her family and marriage.

Scripture Memorization

1 Corinthians 6:19 — Or do you not know that your body is a temple of the Holy Spirit within you, whom you have from God? You are not your own.

Reflection Questions

1. Why do you think it is so important for us to give our lives back to Christ?

2. What words equate with a *temple*?

3. What does a completely surrendered life look like?

4. What does a completely surrendered marriage look like?

ACTIVITY: MISSION MARRIAGE

Journal prompt: Giving my life to God and not being in control feels...

As humans we all search for purpose on earth, but have you thought about your purpose in marriage? As we learned earlier, marriage done God's way is not just for our personal satisfaction—it is a union that should be used by God. A great biblical example of a couple pursuing their life's purpose and God's mission are Aquila and Pricilla. They worked alongside Paul, and he describes them as his "fellow workers in Christ Jesus" (Romans 16:3). They were obviously very instrumental together, as they are mentioned several times.

- **Acts 18:1-3:** After this Paul left Athens and went to Corinth. And he found a Jew named Aquila, a native of Pontus, recently come from Italy and his wife Priscilla, because Claudius had commanded all the Jews to leave Rome. And he went to see them, and because he was of the same trade he stayed with them and worked, for they were tentmakers by trade.
- **Acts 18:18:** After this, Paul stayed many days longer and then took leave of the brothers and set sail for Syria, and with him Priscilla and Aquila. At Cenchreae he had cut his hair, for he was under a vow.
- **Acts 18:26:** He began to speak boldly in the synagogue, but when Priscilla and Aquila heard him, they took him aside and explained to him the way of God more accurately.
- **Romans 16:3-4:** Greet Priscilla and Aquila, my co-workers in Christ Jesus, who risked their necks for my life, to whom not only I give thanks but all the churches of the Gentiles give thanks as well.
- **1 Corinthians 16:19:** The churches of Asia send you greetings. Aquila and Prisca, together with the church in their house, send you hearty greetings in the Lord.
- **2 Timothy 4:19:** Greet Priscilla and Aquila and the household of Onesiphorus.

MY MARRIAGE MISSION

Isn't it refreshing to see a biblical example of a godly marriage? Imagine what their mission statement was like for their marriage. You already have some experience with writing mission statements. Below, write a mission for your marriage. Just as having a life mission statement is a smart way to keep your ultimate long-term life goals in focus, the same goes for a marriage mission.

Of course, when your husband comes along, you will tweak it to fit both your desires, but keep it somewhere you can find it, as it will be fun to see if you were on similar pages!

Pray for God's will to be done in your life, above your own.

John 12:25 I Matthew 10:39 I Acts 20:24 I 1 Corinthians 6:19–20

Monthly Check-in

Did I keep up with my God-plan this month?

How can I make sure that I am not just living for self?

What is my strategy for keeping the mission God gives me in marriage at the forefront?

Is there anything positive that has occurred as a result of my studies or closer connection with God this month?

TESTIMONY TO SHARE:

Notes

www.ingramcontent.com/pod-product-compliance
Lightning Source LLC
Chambersburg PA
CGHW080912170426
LVCB00017B/2301